A
THOUSAND
SMALL
SANITIES

A THOUSAND SMALL SANITIES

THE MORAL ADVENTURE *of* LIBERALISM

ADAM GOPNIK

BASIC BOOKS
New York

Basic Books
Hachette Book Group
1290 Avenue of the Americas, New York, NY 10104
www.basicbooks.com

Printed in the United States of America

First Edition: May 2019

Published by Basic Books, an imprint of Perseus Books, LLC, a subsidiary of Hachette Book
Group, Inc. The Basic Books name and logo is a trademark of the Hachette Book Group.

The Hachette Speakers Bureau provides a wide range of authors for speaking events.
To find out more, go to www.hachettespeakersbureau.com or call (866) 376-6591.

The publisher is not responsible for websites (or their content) that are not owned
by the publisher.

Editorial production by Christine Marra, Marrathon Production Services.
www.marrathoneditorial.org

Book design by Jane Raese
Set in 11-point New Baskerville

Library of Congress Control Number: 2018968456

ISBN 978-1-5416-9936-6 (hardcover); ISBN 978-1-5416-9935-9 (ebook)

LSC-C

10   9   8   7   6   5   4   3   2   1

For Olivia and Luke, as ever,
though this time even more urgently.

And for my father,
who taught me all this, and lives it.

CONTENTS

A
THOUSAND
SMALL
SANITIES

A LONG WALK WITH A
SMART DAUGHTER

ON THE night of the November 2016 election, my seventeen-year-old daughter Olivia, politically aware and intelligently skeptical of all progressive pieties, particularly her father's, was so shocked and troubled by the result that I put my arm around her and together we went for a long walk in the early morning hours around our New York neighborhood. I tried to give her a hopeful attitude in a startling moment. I explained to her why the liberal and humanist values that she had been brought up with were not just some family legacy of attitudes, and attitudinizing, but ideals that were made reliable by experience and proven true by history. I reassured her that democracy flowed from the ground up, and as long as the space of common action was available, no one bad leader could affect it. I showed her how to connect the remote and dry and sterile-seeming ideas that she was learning in history class with the crisis we were now in and how some of those ideas might even show us the way out. She came back home with her spine stiffened and her hopes a little higher.

Well, obviously not. Like every parent on every such occasion, I stumbled and sought for words and didn't find them and found instead my arm around her shoulder and hers around mine. (I am a short man, and she is already my height.) My actual words were, of course, much less confident, or clear, or ambitious—even a middle-aged essayist with a taste for epigrams couldn't claim any kind of aphoristic subtlety, not on a night of such discordance. She needed—we needed—simply to connect. (I noted that she felt better when she turned back, inevitably, to her cell phone and its firecracker explosions of distraught emotion from her ever-encircling—and endlessly texting—friends).

She wasn't shocked because of the rise to power of an opposition party—or if she had been I wouldn't have been particularly sympathetic, the oscillation of parties in power in a democracy being as natural as rain. No, she was shocked by the sudden appearance in her life of the specter of an oafish (and, not incidentally, predatory) authoritarianism, suddenly threatening to annihilate the system of values that she had been brought up to respect. It wasn't that her team lost. It was that for the first time in her life—in my life, too—the rules of the democratic game seemed under assault.

In the years since, as she has gone on to graduate from high school, things have only become more frightening, and the liberal tradition in still greater danger. It isn't just an issue of the survival of "democracy"—after all Iran and Russia are both ostensibly democratic. It is the practice of *liberal* democracy, that magical marriage of free individuals and fair laws—of the pursuit of happiness, each to her own joy, with the practice of disinterested justice, everyone treated the same.

Everywhere we look, throughout Europe as much as in America, patriotism is being replaced with nationalism, pluralism by tribalism, impersonal justice by the tyrannical whim of autocrats who think only to punish their enemies and reward their hitmen. Many of these have gained power by democratic means, but they have kept power by illiberal ones. The death of liberal democracy is announced now with the same certainty that its triumph was proclaimed a mere twenty years before. If in America the authoritarian nightmare has so far turned out to be more like *Goodfellas* than *1984*—well, as the fine film *The Death of Stalin* showed us, *Goodfellas* in power was *exactly* what the evilest kind of authoritarianism could look like.

Yet where could one find for her a real and unapologetic contemporary defense of liberalism? What *is* liberalism, even? In America it means, vaguely, the politics of the center of the Democratic Party. For nostalgics, it means Barack Obama. For nostalgic depressives, it can mean Michael Dukakis. (For despairing nostalgic depressives, it can mean Michael Dukakis in a tank.) Though in Canada liberals unafraid to be called so are often in power, in Britain, the liberal temperament has been largely hived off to the right wing of Labour and the left wing of the Conservative Party. In France what's called liberalism is actually more like what we call libertarianism, while the same tradition that produces our liberalism is more often called republicanism (which, of course, has nothing to do with what we call Republicanism).

Well, words change meaning all the time, over time, and in different places. But whatever liberalism is, no one likes it. In right-wing polemics, liberals are conflated with true left-wing radicals (who, in fact, hate liberals every bit as much as the right wing does, even if the right often misses this). And so, a nonexistent imaginary monster, the left-liberal, is invented. (It's pretty much guaranteed that any time you see that creature, the left-liberal, all serious argument will vanish in its wake.) Among the actual left, the liberal becomes still another imaginary monster, the dreaded neoliberal. If, to borrow a conception from Lewis Carroll's great poem "The Hunting of the Snark" (where there are two monsters, one bad, the other worse, being pursued by a strange Carrollian hunting party), the left-liberal of right-wing polemics is a Snark, a hideous creature, then the neoliberal of left-wing imagination is actually a Boojum—a creature so horrible that it can hardly be glimpsed or identified.

Historically and still today, both the far left and the far right hate liberals more even than they hate their opposite extreme, with whom they share—even if they don't recognize it—a common ground of absolutism. Dogmatic Catholics can speak more readily to dogmatic Communists than to lifelong compromisers. Competing absolutisms respect each other more than either respects those who are allergic to absolutes as an absolute principle.

Liberals are, in the insistent imagination of their enemies, not merely wrong but craven, spineless. They seek centrist solutions to problems that demand radical measures, defend an indefensible status quo—whether that status quo is imagined as one of statist interference or of free-market folly—have no fixed axioms to argue from, and generally collapse, wringing their hands in impotent worry, when trouble starts. There are no atheists in foxholes, and no liberals in bar fights, and what we have today, the insistent sneering insists, is a long permanent bar fight, where you can't trust a liberal to throw a bourbon bottle at the bad guys, whichever bad guys you happen to be aiming bourbon bottles at. Liberals are out-of-touch elitists, at once moralists *and* hedonists. In the middle of the bar fight, the liberal is writing a blog post about biodegradable bottles or, more likely, trying to start a tasting of artisanal bourbons.

Even if you pick up a standard political history, you'll get a more complicated but, in its way, equally uninspiring view of the liberal tradition. It will tend to emphasize the seventeenth- and eighteenth-century European political philosophers Montesquieu and Locke and, sometimes, Hobbes. It will tend to make a great deal about liberal ideas that are contractual and procedural and utilitarian and offer specific social rules, like the rules on a board game box—or else try to calculate how maximal pleasure can be offered to maximum numbers of people. It will offer a vision of liberalism that, in a certain way, is atomized and tends to honor individuals above communities and societies. You'll read about how much liberalism depends on a particular modern and materialist and indeed capitalist idea of individual enterprise, of a spiritually isolated individual who's largely set apart from community and tradition. Robinson Crusoe is sometimes thought of as the original liberal man. Alone on an island, keeping his accounts, planning his future—and, maybe not at all accidentally, depending on a native bearer and manservant for his well-being.

Now, none of this is entirely false. But I don't think it gives us a complete or remotely contemporary picture of the liberal tradition, or of what liberalism means to us, or of what liberalism can become. A distinct idea of a liberal tradition exists and is one we can use and understand. It's really very much in line with the way we use the term in our ordinary speech—to reference people and parties with an equal commitment to reform and to liberty, who want both greater equality among men and women and an ever-greater tolerance for difference among them too.

As an essayist, I have written innumerable—some would say interminable—essays on liberal thinkers and makers and have lived imaginatively among liberal philosophers and politicians and activists and even saints, rather than narrowly with only liberal ideas. My idea of liberalism, while having much to do with individuals and their liberties, has even more to do with couples and communities. We can't have an idea of individual liberty without an idea of shared values that include it.

A vision of liberalism that doesn't concentrate too narrowly on individuals and their contracts but instead on loving relationships and living values can give us a better picture of liberal thought as it's actually evolved than the orthodox picture can. It's a myth, as a new generation of scholars has shown, that liberalism is obsessed with individualism, a myth that liberalism doesn't have a rich imagination of common fates and shared values. Adam Smith, though today he's been appropriated to right-wing think tanks and even right-wing neckties—Milton Friedman always wore one—thought in terms of cities and of how they share sentiments before he thought of individuals and how they price goods.

The great eighteenth-century French philosopher Voltaire, the sage of the Enlightenment, whose tight, complacent smile is a symbol of reason, is a very problematic example of an advocate of liberal democracy in our sense—but he remains an apostle of a kind for having risked his life and welfare for a series of humane reforms, particularly protesting the regal habit of stripping men naked and tearing them apart limb from limb, or breaking their bones in public one at a time with a sledgehammer. Wherever there is a movement for humane reform there is always a liberal around somewhere. Many of the great movements for humane reform—the antislavery crusade, for instance—have also nestled in the bosom of the churches. But in every case, there have been other pious people arguing just as strongly for the opposite view. It enraged the great Frederick Douglass, a sincere Christian, that far more Christian ministers were arguing *for* slavery than against it. The difference was that, on Douglass's side, the right side, there was usually a secular, political liberal or two lurking. (The admixture of Christian piety and liberal principle can, historically, be an extremely potent one, as neither group should forget, though both do.)

⊰◈⊱

Images illuminate ideas, and pictures of people are usually clearer than statements of principle. When I think about the liberal tradition I wanted to show my daughter, my inner vision kept returning to a simple scene, one that had delighted me for a long time. It's of the nineteenth-century philosopher John Stuart Mill and his lover, collaborator, and (as he always insisted) his most important teacher, the writer Harriet Taylor. Desperately in love, they were courting clandestinely, and they would meet secretly at the rhino's cage at the London Zoo. "Our old friend Rhino," Taylor called him in a note. It was a place where they could safely meet and talk without fear of being seen by too many people, everyone's attention being engaged by the enormous exotic animal.

7

They were pained, uncertain, contemplating adultery, if not yet having committed it—opinions vary; they had been to Paris together—and yet in those conversations began the material of "On Liberty," one of the greatest books of political theory ever written, and "On the Subjection of Women," one of the first great feminist manifestos and one of the most explosive books ever written. (One of the most successful, too, inasmuch as almost all of its dreams for female equality have been achieved, at least legally, in our lifetime.)

Throughout his life, Mill said, emphatically and clearly and unambiguously, that Taylor was the smartest person he had ever met and the greatest influence on his work he had ever known. He praised her in terms so superlative they sounded to later readers a little fishy: "Alike in the highest regions of speculation and in the smaller practical concerns of daily life, her mind was the same perfect instrument, piercing to the very heart and marrow of the matter; always seizing the essential idea or principle." And so, after his life, generations of commentators—including Friedrich Hayek, who unfortunately edited their letters—aggressively Yoko-ed her, insisting that poor Mill, wildly intelligent in all but this, was so blinded and besotted by love that he vastly exaggerated the woman's role, which obviously couldn't have been as significant as his own. Fortunately, newer generations of scholars, less blinded by prejudice, have begun to "recover" Harriet Taylor for us, and her role in the making of modern liberalism seems just as large and her mind as fine as her husband always asserted that it was.

Theirs was a complicated lobster quadrille of love. When they met, at a dinner party in Finsbury in 1830, Mill, for all the dry and unsmiling Victorian surface we see in his photographs, was primed for passion. As a boy, Mill had been raised by his father, the great Utilitarian philosopher James Mill, to think of life in something like accounting book terms, with efforts going out and utilities, or pleasures, coming in. But after a horrific nervous breakdown as a young man, Mill turned decisively toward the liberal arts for all his meanings. Mozart knew things that his dad did not. He borrowed the term *self-development* from the German Romantic philosopher Wilhelm von Humboldt and came to consider that, rather than utilitarian pleasure, to be the goal of life.

Taylor, a year younger than Mill, was married to a slow-witted, well-meaning pharmacist named John Taylor; they had two children. She was smart and pretty—"a small head, a swan-like throat, and a complexion like a pearl," the daughter of someone present at the momentous dinner wrote later—and already oppressed by her very unequal marriage. She and Mill fell for each other quickly and began working together. Within a year of their first meeting, someone asked her, concerning a review of Byron, "Did you or Mill do it?" The couple was soon seen everywhere—one reason, again, they sought out the rhino's cage. Thomas Carlyle's wife, Jane, gossiped that "Mrs. Taylor, tho' encumbered with a husband and children, has ogled John Mill so successfully that he was desperately in love." After years of intrigue, the Taylors finally decided on a separation. That was when Harriet went to Paris and, to test Mill's love, invited him to spend six weeks with her there. The interlude was splendid—but then Harriet, with a rather sweet imperiousness, allowed her husband to come to Paris for his own audition. Harriet ultimately decided—with mingled

propriety, uncertainty, and something like flirtatiousness—
that they could share her, on an alternating schedule, at the
Taylor house, her husband entertaining guests with her on
some days, and Mill on others. Taylor paid the bills, while
Mill stocked the wine cellar. (Though in his memoir Mill de-
nied that they had had sex before they were married, there
are purring letters that suggest the contrary. "While you can
love me as you so sweetly & beautifully shewed in that hour
yesterday, I have all I care for or desire," he wrote in one
letter. "The influence of that dear little hour has kept me in
spirits ever since.")

Harriet's own writing of the 1830s and '40s on the oppression of marriage has the urgency of immediate experience. A smart woman who had been obliged to be
someone's idea of a wife, she had sat at too many dinner
tables and watched women dealing with the dumb little dic-
tators: "The most insignificant of men, the man who can
obtain influence or consideration nowhere else, finds one
place where he is chief and head. There is one person, often greatly his superior in understanding, who is obliged
to consult him, and whom he is not obliged to consult. He
is judge, magistrate, ruler, over their joint concerns." Mill
and Taylor, in their later collaborations, most famously in
that 1869 "The Subjection of Women," published after her
death but with her imprint all over it, weren't content to
show that women would be happier if freer; they went right
to the ground and asked what reason we have for thinking
that *any* restraint on women's freedom is just. Mill and Taylor together make the point again and again that no one
can possibly know what women are or are not "naturally"
good at, since their opportunities have been so vanishingly

small compared with the length of their oppression. Arguing against the notion that women have no talent for the fine arts, Mill makes the shrewd point that in the one liberal art where women *are* encouraged as much as men, acting on the stage, everyone admits that they're just as good or better. On a list of modern words that changed the most lives, those which Mill and Taylor wrought together in "The Subjection of Women" must rank high. Before it, women were for all intents and purposes chattel; afterward, they would sooner or later have to be made citizens. You could argue against it, try to unmake it, but you couldn't ignore it. The beach was taken, and the cautious odd couple by the rhino's cage had taken it.

John and Harriet's intellectual idyll was long-lived in shadow, short-lived in sunlight. Mr. Taylor died in 1849, and in 1851 John and Harriet were married. But after only seven and a half years, Harriet died of one of those sad, unnamed wasting diseases that blighted the period. Mill had a monument—made of the same Carrara marble as Michelangelo's *David*—constructed for her in Avignon, with an inscription that included the lines "Were there but a few hearts and intellects like hers / this earth would already become the hoped-for heaven."

At the time of her death, the ideas that John and Harriet began to evolve on that bench by the rhino's cage—on absolute equality for women, on absolute freedom even for the most blasphemous speech—were regarded as not much more than a crazy fantasy. People who try to turn Mill into a cautious centrist disfigure his legacy, and Taylor's, which was entirely radical. Taylor and Mill believed in complete equality of the sexes before anyone else did, just as he believed in the absolute moral evil of slavery while others in Britain were still temporizing. (He did as much as anyone to make the American Civil War won by the right side by enlisting the mill workers of Britain to reject processing cotton from the Confederacy, at some cost to their own immediate interests.)

No, the last thing in the world that this couple by the rhino's cage were was centrists. What they were was realists—radicals of the real, determined to live in the world even as they altered it. Not reluctant realists, but romantic realists. They were shocked and delighted at how quickly women and men began to meet and organize on the theme of women's emancipation, but they accepted that progress would be slow and uncertain and sometimes backward facing. They did more than accept this necessity. They rejoiced in it because they understood that without a process of public argument and debate, of social action moved from below, the ground of women's emancipation would never be fully owned by women nor accepted, even grudgingly, by men.

They had no illusions about their own perfection—they were imperfect, divided people and went on being so for the rest of their lives, with the rueful knowledge of human contradiction that good people always have. Harriet loved John Mill, but stayed with her well-meaning, helpless husband and nursed him through a horrific terminal cancer, in a time before even the horrible treatments we have now. Only after he died did John and Harriet marry, lovingly but all too briefly.

Theirs is one of the most lyrical love stories ever told, for being so tenderly irresolute. Recognizing that intimate

life is an accommodation of contradictions, they understood that political and social life must be an accommodation of contradictions too. The accommodation was their
romance. That meant that social accommodation could be
romantic, too. Love, like liberty, tugs us in different directions as much as it leads us in one. Love, like liberty, asks
us to be only ourselves, and it also asks us to find our self
in others' eyes. Compromise is not a sign of the collapse of
one's moral conscience. It is a sign of its strength, for there
is nothing more necessary to a moral conscience than the
recognition that other people have one, too. A compromise
is a knot tied tight between competing decencies. Harriet
Taylor's love for John Mill was bounded by John Taylor's
pathos and by his love for her. And, since no two moral con-
sciences can go just alike, they have to only be imperfectly
synchronized. Close enough is good enough—for now.

In the very month of Harriet's death in 1858, Mill sent
off to the publisher the finished manuscript of "On Liberty," dedicating it to the memory of "the friend and wife
whose exalted sense of truth and right was my strongest
incitement." The romance in Mill's life helped turn him
from a thinking machine into a feeling mensch; the know-
it-all became an anything-for-love. The great relationship
of his life would be proof of his confidence that true liberty
meant love—relationship and connection, not isolation and
self-seeking. What we want liberty *for* is the power to connect with others as we choose. Liberalism is our common
practice of connection turned into a principle of pluralism,
teenage texting raised to the power of law.

It dawned on me while I brooded on the long-dead rhino
in his long-gone cage that the rhinoceros was the perfect

symbol of liberalism. All living things, Darwin taught us, are compromises of a kind, the best that can be done for that moment between the demands of the environment and the genetic inheritance it has to work with. No living thing is ideal. A rhinoceros is just a big pig with a horn on it.

The ideal of the unicorn is derived from the fact of the rhinoceros—the dream image of the rhinoceros, the single horned animal reported on and then idealized by the medieval imagination. People idealize unicorns and imagine unicorns and make icons out of unicorns and write fables about unicorns. We hunt them. They're perfect. The only trouble with them is that they do not exist. They never have. The rhino is ungainly and ugly and short-legged and imperfect and squat. But the rhinoceros is real. It exists. And it is formidable.

Most political visions are unicorns, perfect imaginary creatures we chase and will never find. Liberalism is a rhinoceros. It's hard to love. It's funny to look at. It isn't pretty but it's a completely successful animal. A rhino can overturn an SUV and—go to YouTube!—run it right over, horn out.

❧

So, the critical liberal words are not *liberty* and *democracy* alone—vital though they are—but also *humanity* and *reform, tolerance* and *pluralism, self-realization* and *autonomy,* the vocabulary of passionate connection and self-chosen community. These are hardly uncontroversial or simple concepts, either. But they point to a range of specific public ambitions and policies—the humane reform of prisons, of punishments, of making luncheonettes open to all and leaving decisions about how many children to have to the woman who has to have them—that all have as their end eliminating cruelty and sadism and needless suffering from the world.

Liberalism *ends* in the center not because that's where liberals always think the sanity is, but because they recognize that there are so many selves in a society that must be accommodated that you can't expect them to congregate in a single neighborhood at one end or another of the city. The meeting place, the piazza, in an Italian village, is placed in the center of the town because everyone can get there. The ancient Greeks thought of this meeting place as the "agora," which meant the market but meant more broadly the place where citizens met for unplanned meetings. Tyrants of all kinds, Persian and Spartan, feared the agora in the most literal way, and tried to eliminate it from their cities.

We can follow the standard, orthodox histories of liberalism in dating it back to the seventeenth century, and we can certainly see its outlines in the eighteenth-century Enlightenment. But it's in the 1860s, precisely in John and Harriet's wake, that recognizably modern liberalism, as a practice and fulfilled temperament, is established. It happens in a stunningly short time frame, from 1859 to 1872: through the American Civil War to just past the establishment of the Third Republic in Paris. In that period, there appeared the two foundational documents of modern liberal humanism, Darwin's *On the Origin of Species* and Mill's *On Liberty*. Darwin's was a new articulation of the history of life and humanity's place within it, implicit but obvious, and Mill's was the articulation of a new understanding about the nature of authority and the individual's claims against it.

On the political front, the long decade of modern liberalism's birth witnessed the enfranchisement of most of the British working classes, the formal founding of the British Liberal Party (headquartered in the London Reform Club, no less), the absolute victory of the antislavery (and single-nation) side in the American Civil War, and the founding, after the disaster of the French commune, of the French Republic in the form in which, with the interruption of the German occupation, it has essentially persisted since. (And let us not forget, in 1867, the establishment of the Canadian confederation and of a still unprecedented, in its survival and tensile strength, bilingual and binational nation.) All these events are linked: it was the victory of the Union that helped prod the democratization of Britain, and the vindication of republicanism in the United States and Britain that played a large role in re-moralizing the French republicans. (It was the same period that saw, as well, the emergence of liberalism's great opponents: authoritarian nationalism, with Bismarck's unification of Germany in 1871, and radical socialism, with the first meeting of the Workingmen's Association, under the influence of Karl Marx, in London in 1864.)

The greatest monument of modern liberalism began precisely in that hour, too, as a gift from nascent French republicanism to triumphant American republicanism. We have allowed the Statue of Liberty to be subsumed into the narrative of American immigration, and understandably so given that for many millions of American ancestors this French thing was the first American thing they saw. But it was first imagined, in that pivot year of 1865, as a tribute to the shining light of the republican ideal at a time when it still seemed impossible in France. It was an imaginary dream figure celebrating the vindication of liberty in America with an eye to its eventual vindication in France: you've married her; we will, too, some day. She is a figure of that crucial long decade, in which modern liberalism is mostly forged.

The hallucinatory photographs of the statue rising in a small Parisian atelier remind us of its binational nature—and also of its impossible conception. It ought to be, like the dream of liberal democracy itself, left in the large dustbin of unrealized projects, like Tatlin's later Monument to the Third International. It isn't. It's there. It shines. Britain, France, and America in that short decade became, or were on their way to becoming, liberal democracies in ways they had not been before.

The dreams of liberalism, of republicanism, of far-reaching reform were very imperfectly realized. The world is an imperfect place, and liberals are imperfect actors within it. But new social practices rose, like the statue, against a background in which it was quite possible to imagine, in 1859, that *none* of it could happen—that slave power would win in North America, that reaction would triumph in Britain, and that an empire or monarchy was the likeliest future for France. Instead, one got liberal reformist regimes, which, for all their failings and faults, under William Ewart Gladstone and Ulysses S. Grant and Léon Gambetta, established governments that we can recognize as like our own and societies that look like ours, from Christmas cards and department stores to the first serious stirrings of women's rights.

The liberalism that began then isn't at all like the rules on the back of a board game. It tends to hold implicit and explicit ideas about community, reform, violence, sexual roles, and more. Liberalism, in the specific sense that I wanted to explain to my daughter, is an attempt to *realize* liberty, not merely to invoke it or make it the subject of an incantation.

For liberals use the word *liberty* the way the word love is used by songwriters—it's what the song leads to but not all the song can be. Merely being in favor of liberty is like being in favor of love—everyone is, and nothing is solved by it, as John and Harriet were wise enough to know. It's the other words around it that make the key word matter. Tony Bennett said once that you should always pay special attention when Frank Sinatra sings the word *love*. But that's because love is not the only word he sings.

That's the heart of what I wanted to tell you, Olivia. That the search for radical change by humane measures, far from producing a dry, atomizing, and emotion-less doctrine in which all social relations are reduced to the status of a contract, makes liberalism one of the great moral adventures in human history. Far from being fatuously materialistic, merely gross, and profit driven, the rise and triumph of liberal ideas is the most singular spiritual episode in all of human history. There was little like it in human history before—the ancients did imagine a world without divinity but nothing like the moral scope of the emancipation from cruelty of slaves and women.

Liberalism is a fact-first philosophy with a feelings-first history. Liberal humanism is a whole, in which the humanism always precedes the liberalism. Powerful new feelings about a compassionate connection to other people, about community, have always been informally shared before they are crystallized into law. Social contacts precede the social contract. Understanding the emotional underpinnings of liberalism is essential to understanding its political project. Its history is merely material in the same way that the action of great novels is merely material. The model liberal person is less like lonely, account-mad Robinson Crusoe and a lot closer to Elizabeth Bennet in *Pride and Prejudice*, living every day within an inescapable family structure and specific social ground but trying to negotiate a new role for herself through intelligence and argument and wit. Lizzy Bennet recognizes that the ground of the social arrangement is not going to be completely remade by a single marriage, but she is willing to stand up to Lady Catherine de Bourgh and against the whole aristocratic order, in defense of her own pursuit of happiness. Liberalism is realistic about the huge task of remaking worlds. But it is romantic about the possibility of making marginally happier endings for as many as possible within this one.

To offer a liberal credo, however, also means to offer as fair and even as eloquent an account as I can of the *attacks* on liberalism, from both left and right. Because freedom of *debate*, even more than freedom of speech, is central to the liberal ideal, a liberal credo without counterarguments becomes just another dogma. God knows there is no shortage of attacks to draw on. You, Olivia, offered one that night, and over the next year, one set of objections after another, which struck the inner ear of my imagination. Of course, you're a liberal, you told me! Yes, in the same way that a coal miner is in favor of coal and the Prince of Wales a monarchist. You benefit from its institutions and therefore think them swell. It's not an accident that the fullest throated defenders of the rigging of the existing order are middle-aged white men who have benefited from the way it's rigged. Find me a black man or woman, a Latino kid, who isn't far more suspicious of and hostile to the liberal (or neoliberal) world order, and I will be impressed. People always find elaborate ways to defend their own privileges. Everyone sees what they like in the dispensation they've inherited and sticks to it on pretended principle. Colonialism was the working face of liberalism in Africa, and CIA coups were the working face of liberalism in South America. Institutionalized racism, the scandal of mass incarceration, is another face of the liberal order, the orange jumpsuit beneath the cosmetic skin.

A liberalism that doesn't offer hope to Ecuadorian peasants and Haitian sweatshop workers and Congolese children caught in cobalt mines as much as it does for Manhattan progressive families is hardly worth defending but just one more paper sign stuck up over the family shop. These arguments, cries for human empathy, resonate in our life from all of those who have gone out to bear witness to the suffering of others, or who have borne witness by being themselves the sufferers, from Frederick Douglass to Alexander Berkman. And meanwhile, the right-wing arguments—for authority against liberal relativism and for the integrity of communities against liberal cosmopolitanism—were ones I have come to know well through a lifetime of reading, most often found in authors who I loved like brothers, or uncles—sometimes crazy uncles—from Samuel Johnson to G. K. Chesterton.

Liberalism is as distinct a tradition as exists in political history, but it suffers from being a practice before it is an ideology, a temperament and a tone and a way of managing the world more than a fixed set of beliefs. (At least this means that poets and novelists and painters, a Trollope or a George Eliot or a Manet, can be better guides to its truths than political philosophers or pundits.) It also presents a paradox: supposedly the most impersonal of ideologies, liberalism depends most on personal example. Liberal people have made liberalism. A liberal credo without characters and action is not only hard to love, it is also impossible to *see*. I wanted you to watch people as they lived as much as hear the principles those people spoke. I wanted you to meet Taylor and Mill by the rhino's cage. I wanted you to encounter some other unorthodox liberal lovers, George Eliot and George Lewes, as they, in that same London and sometimes at that same zoo, later on tried to reconcile Darwinism with humanism. I wanted you to see André Glucksmann's mother saving her family's life by daring to tell the truth to the other Jewish deportees at Drancy in 1941, setting her son free to journey, as a Parisian intellectual, from murderous Maoism to modest humanism. I wanted you to meet Bayard Rustin, the great black and gay man who organized the march on Washington in 1963 and who, at the end of his long life, summed up his credo elegantly in the three simplest of distinctly liberal dance positions: "1) nonviolent tactics; 2) constitutional means; 3) democratic procedures." And I wanted you to know the counterpoised personalities, too. I wanted you to learn from the passion of Emma Goldman and see the point of Edmund Burke.

By making liberalism a subject of persons and places, as much as of principles, perhaps I can help to humanize it again for a new generation. Perhaps I can make those who have benefited from its graces hate its vices, which are large, just a bit less and see its virtues, even larger, just a bit more clearly. I might even be able to show why the happiness of the world depends—no, we are liberals and can say only *may* depend—on its renewal. I still think it's a walk worth taking, and a talk worth having.

∿ CHAPTER ONE ∿

THE RHINOCEROS MANIFESTO: WHAT IS LIBERALISM?

POTENT SENTENCES can take peculiar forms. In the very last chapter of *The Descent of Man*, Charles Darwin writes coolly, with seeming descriptive objectivity, that "we thus learn that man is descended from a hairy quadruped, furnished with a tail and pointed ears, probably arboreal in its habits, and an inhabitant of the Old World." It is probably the most explosive sentence ever written in English, overthrowing millennia of belief in the unique and divine creation of man, but it comes at us so quietly and at such comically detailed length that it is hard for us to quite believe how slyly provocative it is.

Liberalism has many mouths, but the liberalism that those of us who think of ourselves as liberal humanists want to defend—opposed both to the leftists with whom we sometimes make common cause and the right wing with which we sometimes share common premises—has one true point, equally potent, equally plain. *Liberalism is an evolving political practice that makes the case for the necessity and possibility of (imperfectly) egalitarian social reform and ever greater (if not absolute) tolerance of human difference through reasoned and (mostly) unimpeded conversation, demonstration, and debate.*

That sentence is, I'm aware, anticlimactic and possibly uninspiring to the point of fatuity, not to mention rage. It's an *infuriating* sentence! I doubt that I've ever put down a clumsier one. "I am for freeing man from his chains!" the Marxist ideologue hails. "I am for faith and family!" the Christian warrior proclaims. "I am for an ongoing belief in the need for nonviolent incremental alterations of existing institutions and an all-around effort to be nicer to everyone!" the liberal tries to cry out—and then can only sigh. The slogan won't even fit on a banner.

Yet that sentence, composed clause by clause over centuries by generations of liberal minds, like stonemasons working on the façade of a cathedral, has, I think, consequences that make it as explosive as Darwin's. It's a rhino of a sentence, yes, but each of its ugly clauses enfolds some huge advance in moral understanding and effective action. Liberalism depends on shadings and qualifications, on "evolvings" and "imperfectlies." It has a soft and awkward rhetoric. Like the rhino, it aggravates by its ungainliness. Yet what liberalism has in its favor are the facts. Liberals get nothing accomplished—except everything, eventually. In Western Europe, in America, certainly in Canada, in Australia, too, vistas of general legal and social equality far outstripping anything previously known to mankind, and largely achieved by peaceful and parliamentary means, have been won.

That these new vistas of equality are under assault now does not alter the scale of the accomplishment. When we get a Social Security check, or attend a gay friend's marriage, or simply exercise the right to vote as a woman or hold office as a Jew or Mormon, we are the beneficiaries of Bayard Rustin's three simple dance steps of liberalism. We may see, and say, for instance, that LGBTQ rights are being attacked in America by a revanchist right wing—but we need also to stop and think that the very idea that these capital letters would enclose a party of people who have rights worth protecting is entirely and exclusively a recent invention of liberal countries. (Homosexuality has flourished elsewhere—it is part of the human condition—but has *never* been specifically protected and even nurtured before as it is now even in the public high schools of New York.)

Militant activism was certainly responsible for the achievement of many of these reforms. But it was specifically *liberal* activism. It wasn't trying to change everything at once. It was trying to fix what was wrong now. Civil disobedience, women chaining themselves to parliament fences, the bravery of the Chartists in Britain or the Popular Front in France or the Selma marchers—all are part of the story of human self-liberation. But in the end their goals were specific, not utopian, capable of being achieved by democratic means in democratic legislatures, even if only when the cost of not achieving them became too great for the powers already in place.

But feelings move people more than arguments. That liberal sentence is complicated and unwieldy because it expresses the evolution over a long period of time of new values: a hatred of brutality, a recognition of the primacy of sympathy as social cement, a feeling for normal frailty and for mercy before justice and humanity before dogma, a desire, so to speak, to systematize compassion and put the brakes on normal human cruelty. How these feelings happened is the story of the moral adventure of liberalism.

~~~

The foundation of liberalism is cracked in advance. Modern liberalism—as distinct from earlier and more general meanings of the term as "generous" or "learned"— begins with a psychological principle, a human principle. Its foundation is fallibilism—the truth that we are usually wrong about everything and always divided within ourselves about anything we believe. Reform rather than revolution or repetition is essential because what we are doing now is likely to be based on a bad idea and because what we do next is likely to be bad in some other way too. Incremental cautious reform is likely to get more things right than any other kind.

Now, liberalism has many origins. To be liberal has meant many things over the centuries, and it's good to know the range of things it has meant and evolved from. It's possible to see modern liberalism as an offshoot of in-fighting among seventeenth-century religious dissidents or as a movement in its origins more preoccupied with fighting for national freedom than for universal fairness. It's always enlightening and sometimes inspiring to know how concepts evolved, but we shouldn't commit an originalist fallacy and think that because a term once upon a time meant something it must *really* mean that now. A humanist in the Renaissance meant someone who read Greek and Latin, not someone who is kind to animals or to other people, but that isn't want it means now.

Scientific words often evolve from feeling to knowledge; social words tend to evolve inexorably from knowledge to feeling. Our ancestors talked about lumbago or melancholia, and over time we've come to understand these things better as specific viruses or neurochemical disorders. Our ancestors might at various moments have thought of a liberal as someone with a very specific number of positions on set topics, but we've come to recognize liberalism as a more encompassing emotional temperament. A populist was once someone working for agrarian reform; that isn't the case now. A Republican was once someone who fought for civil rights and now—you see the point. That a word or concept has a history does not make it mean what it once meant. Trees have roots; human beings don't. What they have instead are histories. Histories are ways of thinking about the past and the present, which allow us to imagine new futures.

And so, historically, the first liberal, the founding father if we have one, is the great sixteenth-century French essayist Michel de Montaigne. Montaigne, who lived from 1533 to 1592, wasn't a philosopher or a political pundit; he was a wealthy guy who served two terms as mayor of Bordeaux and invented the essay or *essai*, the French word for "try"—an essay being, in his view, the most human of forms because it is an effort, not an end point. Montaigne the essayist understood how divided we are as human beings, not just how fantastically likely we are to grow away from our ideals but how incompatible our ideals usually are with one another. And that meant we had to base our social behavior on compassion, skepticism, and uncertainty rather than on dogma, justice, and utopianism. He is reputed to have said that, having seen the law at work, if someone had accused him of having stolen the towers of Notre-Dame, he would flee the country rather than stand trial. He knew that abstract justice almost never gets done, certainly not in his time. But he also knew that individual acts of cruelty could stop if people simply stopped doing so many cruel things. That insight marks the beginning of the morality of modern liberalism.

Now, one of the traps of writing manifestoes is that we accede to what I call the Falling Dominoes of Influences. This is the belief, which you find in almost every survey of how we got where we are, that political and social history is the accumulation of big thoughts passed on by big thinkers. Hobbes thought this, Locke thought that, then Rousseau thought something else—and now they won't serve sushi at Oberlin. I have reviewed and read, too often, books blaming Voltaire for everything wrong with the world, and then other books blaming his enemy Rousseau for the same things, or for other things that are wrong with the world now. Of all the kinds of history not worth reading, this kind of intellectual telephone game is often the most fatuous, and its variant, intellectual demonology, where one bad thinker infects the next, the most fatuous of all. You can make Nietzsche and Heidegger into moral monsters who precipitated Hitler or, in the case of Heidegger, collaborated with him, and you can also make a plausible case for them as great philosophers who happened to be taken hostage by bad men.

In truth, *any* thinker big enough to be interesting is also going to be broad enough to double—if not triple or quadruple. There are at least four Marxes, six Kants, and, by my

count, eight credible Voltaires. John Stuart Mill was by turns
a libertarian, a feminist, a capitalist, a rationalist, a mystic,
and a kind of imperialist. All these are elements in the sym-
phony of his work. His ideas aren't necessarily muddled;
it's that people who think for a living are not thought ma-
chines but people. They change their views from day to day,
mood to mood, and circumstance to circumstance—one day
following a secret passage to El Dorado and the next day a
blind alley to Nowheresville. More important, philosophers
and their big ideas are, as often as not, the efflorescence of
their time rather than the cause of it. A big idea usually is
the condensation of many breaths more than it is the wind
that blows history forward. Montaigne and Mill and Taylor
and the others we'll meet crystallized emotions that were
widely shared by large numbers of people who couldn't articulate them as well. Intellectuals bear witness more often
than they make history.

Nonetheless, if Montaigne was not the first to feel the
things he wrote, he was the first to write the things he felt.
He saw, in the late Renaissance, that we are double in ourselves: we condemn the thing we believe and embrace the
thing we condemn. By giving life to this truth, he animates
for the first time an inner human whose contradictions are
identical with his conscience. ("If I speak diversely of myself, it is because I look diversely upon myself," he writes
in "Of the Inconstancy of Our Actions." "All contrarieties
are found in her [the writer's soul] according to some turn
or removing, and in some fashion or other. Shame-faced,
bashful, insolent, chaste, luxurious, peevish, prattling, silent, fond, doting, laborious, nice, delicate, ingenious, slow,
dull, forward, humorous, debonair, wise, ignorant . . . we

are all framed of flaps and patches.") It was from an acceptance of our divided natures—not sinful, necessarily, since
the good bits and the bad bits come from the same whole,
but simply and permanently imperfect—that a new kind of
morality arose. The essential point of Montaigne's great,
foundational essay "On Cruelty," in which he considers the
emotions of a deer being hunted, is that when it comes to
cruelty, we should second all other reasoning to the essential fact of the stag's suffering. We can always rationalize our
way past someone else's suffering. Reasoning past suffering
is not reason at all.

This side of Montaigne's work had an enormous influence on Shakespeare, who read Montaigne in a beautiful
early English translation by John Florio. He adapted his
thoughts on cruelty and put them in the mouth of his wise
misanthropic character Jaques in *As You Like It*. Shakespeare's
divided characters—Hamlet, who has a long, witty conversation about how to be a really good actor and then stabs his
girlfriend's father to death in his mother's bedroom—reflect
Montaigne's new kind of double-minded psychology.

Montaigne is an emotional, not a contractual, liberal.
He didn't give a damn about democracy, or free speech, or
even property rights. They were outside his experience or
his sense of possibility. Even equality before the law he saw
as impossible—not even aristocrats could get it in the regime
under which he lived. That's why he made the crack about
the towers of Notre-Dame. But he had a rich foundational
impulse toward the emotions that make a decent relation
between man and state possible—a far-reaching skepticism
about authority, compassion for those who suffer, and a
hatred of cruelty. We now imagine that these feelings are

instinctual—but all experience shows us that they must be inculcated. Montaigne, having no access to the abstract concepts that were later laid on this foundation, gives us deeper access to them when we read him because he was the first to put down this (cracked) foundation. The liberalism that came after humanism may be what keeps Montaigne's memory alive and draws us to him. The humanism that has to exist before liberalism can even begin is what Montaigne is there to show us still.

Liberalism accepts imperfection as a fact of existence. Some imperfections can be remedied. Many can't. Everything has them. Fixing cruelty is work enough for men and women. Liberalism's task is not to imagine the perfect society and drive us toward it but to point out what's cruel in the society we have now and fix it if we possibly can. An acceptance of fallibility and, with it, an openly avowed skepticism of authority—these are core liberal emotions even more than concerns about checks and balances between the executive and legislative branches.

These were *modern* emotions. Compassion for human flaws is a different emotion than forgiveness for sins. The second presupposes a church capable of offering forgiveness; the first presupposes only a community capable of common feeling. One accepts pain-giving authority; the other painfully acknowledges its absence. Our father forgives us for our trespasses; we forgive each other for our faults. It's why Montaigne says that God can't be virtuous; only people can. Virtue involves the capacity for overcoming our own grievances to look honestly at other people. "Virtue presupposes difficulty," he wrote, in a compressed but epochal phrase.

André Glucksmann, a contemporary French inheritor of Montaigne, offered a similar insight. Glucksmann came from a Jewish family who missed extermination by just this much—his mother got the family out of a deportation camp by telling all the other inmates that they were being sent to be killed. The French police removed them for fear of her inflaming the others.

Glucksmann grew up to be a child of the French revolt of May 1968. He came of age at a time when the anthropologist Claude Lévi-Strauss had made canonic to French structuralism the idea that human culture could be understood through a series of binary oppositions—the difference between what could be eaten raw and what cooked being one of the most fundamental.

Glucksmann, as he matured, came to believe that these crisp binary oppositions were abstractions that sealed us off from the actual lived reality of our ever-muddled existence. So to the simple French structuralist dichotomy of the raw and the cooked, Glucksmann added one more term—the rotting. Most things are rotting and rotten, neither neatly raw nor symbolically cooked. True of food in a literal sense, the truth also applies to human conduct. We know what's rotting by its smell, and our goal can be simply to keep our nurture from spoiling. We don't know what is good, but we do know what is bad. Cruelty is bad. Starvation is bad. State murder is bad. This kind of liberalism extends the French humanist tradition, turning pessimism about "truths" into optimism about acts. As Bernard-Henri Lévy, his colleague and fellow child of '68, puts it, what matters is "the Voltairean idea that successful revolutions turn not on fanatic fidelity to an ideal, but on methodical infidelity to solutions that are prefabricated, final, and, precisely, *ideal*." Fixing the imperfect is enough to do even if we have no idea whatever what the perfect is like. We cannot hope to make mankind less inconsistent, but we can work together to make a world less cruel. We need to hold ourselves to the rhino standard, not the unicorn fantasy—to ask always what's the best real possibility, not what's the ultimate ideal imagining.

∽❦∾

How can you pass from feeling sad when a stag is suffering to actually making saner arrangements about laws and punishments that make people suffer less? How do you go from cultivating compassion to actually making a better world in which, so to speak, compassion can be shared, even compelled? How can you go from a practice of compassion in individual cases—Jaques weeping over the suffering stag—to a principle of peaceful coexistence among kinds? That's the liberal challenge and the liberal conundrum.

This was why, in the middle of the eighteenth century, thinking people in Britain became preoccupied with the way that David Hume was dying. Boswell and Johnson debated it. Other people asked what he was saying as he did. For Hume, a notorious infidel, was, though suffering extremely, reported to be dying in Edinburgh with dignity and self-respect, fearlessly, as if the threat of permanent extinction without a reward in heaven (or punishment in hell) was to him no threat at all. Even Boswell, who wanted desperately to reinforce his own shaky faith with an image of a distressed infidel, had to admit that Hume was "placid and even cheerful . . . talking of different matters with a

33

tranquility of mind and a clearness of head which few men possess at any time." (Dr. Johnson scoffed and said that, of course, having placed his chips on infidelity, Hume would continue to play the hand till the end.)

Frequently at his bedside was another odd Scot: Adam Smith, a carefully closed-mouth writer and teacher, an academic in the modern sense. Hume was his mentor and teacher, and together, among much else, they had insensibly collaborated on a philosophical project—to clarify the primacy of sympathy in creating human connections, making people matter to other people even when the other people were very other.

The idea of sympathy as the glue of good societies is one that began to have an especially intense life in the eighteenth century. Indeed, the idea of sympathy is at least as important to the birth of modern liberalism as the practice of science. What's called the Enlightenment—in France it's called the Lumières, the Enlighteners, a name I like even more—obviously plays an enormously important role in most histories of how liberalism happened, and rightly so. But I think we can miss the most important aspect of the Enlightenment in creating liberal ideas. Most admiring histories of the mid-to-late eighteenth century turn to the glorification and vindication of science and against the clericalism and institutionalized religion that Hume had rejected. The experimental method of science, the argument goes, was the basis for a new faith in reason—and that faith in evidence and argument became the basis for the liberal revolutions of the era.

It was certainly one of the great transformations in human history, one that changed our attitudes for good about the power of hard fact and empirical evidence. But I think it's important to see that the most influential *liberal* thinkers of the Enlightenment were not necessarily the ones who accepted the idea that Reason with a capital R could now explain everything, or that Reason could replace God and become itself a kind of idol. (The French revolutionaries went so far as replacing churches with so-called Temples of Reason, though no one ever quite figured out how to *worship* Reason the way one worshipped Jehovah or Jesus. Reasonable music and rational masses will never stir the believer's blood.) An unthinking reverence for Reason has been rightly criticized and even condemned as oppressive and in its own way crazy. By totalizing our ambitions—making all or nothing solutions seem to be the only rational kind—it became responsible for much mass cruelty, everything from mental institutions to solitary confinement in prisons and colonial racism. It helped make all of those overriding and overarching systems that claimed to be reasonable but that crushed human beings within them.

But in truth the most important liberal thinkers of the era were not the ones who embraced reason uncritically, but exactly the ones who took from the scientific revolution an enormous lesson in skepticism, who saw that one of the things that reasoning really showed was that reason had limits, that you couldn't easily get from a fact to a value, and that you never really know, do you? The two strange Scots turned this kind of skepticism about the power of reasoning to do it all into a positive principle of social sympathy.

They are not conventionally inspiring figures. Adam Smith's biographers have always sighed at his irredeemable dullness; not much happened to him, certainly nothing romantic or even very interesting. His sex life was as dull as oatmeal, and only one really lively anecdote about him survives: at age three he was kidnapped by a tinker, that is, a gypsy, and had to be rescued by his uncle. But the odd thing is that the uneventfulness of his life is part of its modernity: it's just the kind of life that a man with similar gifts and temperament would have now. He scored early by giving good and well-researched lectures under the patronage of an older wise man, became a department chairman, was mentored by older academics, found a fine tenured job at a good university, and then moved into government, until he could make a good living publishing big books while giving the occasional undergraduate survey course.

Hume, in turn, after his early nervous breakdown as a young man—which drove him to France and may well have turned him into a student of Buddhist ideas—was a model of dry Scottish calm, able to soothe or to try and soothe even Gallic temperaments as attenuated as Jean-Jacques Rousseau. But he was about as openly infidel as any man could be in that still straitened time. Though he had a serene temper and would occasionally play transparently ironic lip service to the idea of a creator, Hume hardly made a secret of his atheism or his contempt for organized religion. By the time he reached his deathbed, he was no longer even particularly cautious: "The morality of every religion was bad," he told Boswell flatly. When he heard a man was religious, Hume concluded he was a rascal, though he had known some instances of very good men being religious. The flat statement, and the qualification, are both typical.

In Edinburgh, in the early 1750s, Hume had become Smith's closest friend and his greatest influence but also, in a way, his nemesis: though far from a romantic figure, Hume had an odd core of courage, which both impressed Smith and frightened him a little. For Hume, though in some ways a conventional Enlightenment figure, was also the Enlightenment's greatest skeptic. He saw, and showed, the sharp limits of Reason—and the power of sympathy, rather than either reason or faith, to make humankind one.

Hume, following Shaftsbury, thought that sympathy was the primary human faculty, our key gift. It's the emotional mucilage that brings men and women together and keeps them together. Sex may make us want someone else's company, but that's an animal desire: it's our ability to feel *for* someone, rather than to just, uh, feel them, that makes us human.

Sympathetic feelings are what keep us from being locked in a kind of zombie-like isolation. Sympathy lets us turn ideas into emotions. We don't just think abstractly about somebody else's suffering; we can actually feel it as they do. Sympathy, for Hume, is "the conversion of an idea into an impression [meaning an emotion] by the force of our imaginations." It's why we're more moved by a picture of a single drowned Syrian child—and even moved, we hope, to action—than by a chart showing the number of deaths in Syria. *Everyone* is sooner or later a dying stag, capable of producing a sympathetic feeling in another heart.

Most of Smith's ideas about political economy derive from Hume's. Smith's theory of the flow of balance of trade was Hume's first of all, and Smith's idea that sympathy makes markets work were Hume's too. Yet Smith added something new to the picture. He clinched in practice what Hume saw abstractly. His favorite words, *active* and *productive*, are not at all Hume's words. Smith, though he didn't have much of one by romantic standards, liked life. What Smith took from Hume's demonstration of the limits of reason, the absurdity of superstition, and the primacy of the passions was not a lesson of Buddhist-Stoical indifference but something more like a sense of Epicurean intensity—if we are living in the material world, then let us make it our material.

Smith wrote two great books: the first, *The Theory of Moral Sentiments*, is lesser known; the second, *The Wealth of Nations*, is canonized and even sacralized. Right-wing libertarians have often memorized *The Wealth of Nations* (or the CliffsNotes version anyway) or at least the phrase *invisible hand*—which does actually appear in the book—but without knowing a thing about Smith's theory of morality. In both books, he suggests that it's normal for human beings to want to live in a prosperous society, but that it's also normal for them to want to live in a broadly just society. Their desire for self-improvement was rooted not in greed but sympathy and was inherently social: what we love isn't acquiring alone but haggling, bargaining, interacting, the whole work of building worlds out of wishes. What moved men to make markets was their love of pleasure and happiness. Who, he wondered, could live happily in a society where all of the wealth has been confiscated and kept in a few hands? Smith believed not that markets make men free but that free men move toward markets. The difference is small but decisive; it is most of what we mean by humanism.

Hume's slow and scary death was therefore—as Hume perhaps knew—the test case of his and Smith's kind of humanism: Could a declared infidel face his own annihilation with the same serenity that he had been famous for in his lifetime? Was sympathy enough to keep a skeptic sane? Smith, who kept him company in Edinburgh, was, in effect, Hume's chosen witness, telling the world that Hume's serenity remained, to his dying day, as unbroken as his "infidelity." His atheism remained intact with his aplomb. Just a few days before his death, Hume, joking about begging for a delay from Charon, the ferryman of recently departed souls in Greek mythology, said that "I thought I might say, Good Charon, I have been endeavoring to open the eyes of the people; have a little patience only till I have the pleasure of seeing the churches shut up, and the clergy sent about their business; but Charon would reply, 'O, you loitering rogue. That won't happen these two hundred years.'" With an ironic meaning they could not have known, it was the night of July 4, 1776.

It is the primacy that liberals still place on the kind of fallibility that Montaigne described as foundational to our humanity—the same flawed but not in itself sinful nature that Smith and Hume thought could become the glue of social sympathy—that makes liberals favor reform through what we could call "provoked consensus." The liberal idea of community is not one, as it is for many conservatives, of blood ties or traditional authority. It rests on an idea of shared choices. But the choices, and the sharing, are essential to it, including even a sense of sympathy for those caught on the losing side of an argument. Someone proposes a more equitable world—enfranchisement for working people, blacks, or women, or civil rights for homosexuals—and then makes the resulting reform last by assuring that those who opposed it may have lost the fight but haven't lost their dignity, their autonomy, or their chance to adapt to the change without fearing the loss of all their agency. In this way, liberalism is the most truly radical of all ideologies: it proposes a change, makes it happen, and then makes it last.

That new language of compassionate emotion, trying to think sympathetically about society, tends on the whole to favor *reform* over *revolution*. Liberals believe in reason and reform. But they believe first of all in reform—that the world has many ills, that tradition is a very mixed bag of nice things and nasty things, and that we can work together to fix the nasty ones while making the nice ones available to more people. They believe in reform rather than revolution because the results are in: it works better. More permanent positive social change is made incrementally rather than by revolutionary transformation. This was, originally, something like a temperamental instinct, a preference for social peace bought at a reasonable price, but by now it is a rational preference. The nameable goals of the socialist and even Marxist manifestos of the nineteenth century— public education, free health care, a government role in the economy, votes for women—have all been achieved, mostly peacefully and mostly successfully, by acts of reform in liberal countries. The attempt to achieve them by fiat and command, in the Soviet Union and China and elsewhere, created catastrophes, moral and practical, on a scale still almost impossible to grasp.

An immediate objection strikes us and should. Yes, of course, it's true: the two most famous moves toward what we think of as liberal societies, in America in 1776 and then in France in 1789, both began with revolutions—and bloodier ones, particularly in the American case, than we sometimes remember. The revolution that began just after David Hume died was not an easy act of social sympathy passing among like-minded people. It was a bloody act of warfare imposed by a minority of true believers, the "patriots," on a mostly unenthusiastic population. The blood in the French Revolution came mostly after the revolution was won; in the American attempt, it was the path to victory.

But both happened only after the process of reform was stopped cold by die-hard reactionaries. The Declaration of Independence makes it plain that the founders thought of revolution as a last resort after every other kind of petition had been thwarted, and the actual violent acts of the French Revolution came about simultaneously with an attempt to keep the king in power and move, gradually, toward a more egalitarian society. The revolutionaries in France at first wanted a constitutional monarchy, and only turned to regicide after the king of France and his family, wrongly encouraged by the other reactionary powers, tried to flee.

Liberals are not afraid of revolution. But liberals will remain reluctant revolutionaries. It is one reason why the American Revolution, on the whole, went so much better than the French one—or at least built a society whose foundational documents could be reinterpreted, not replaced. The American Civil War was in essence a second American revolution and could not have been bloodier—but the liberals on the right side of the slavery argument could argue, and did, that the Constitution was on their side, and then what had to be achieved *was* achieved by amending it.

Frederick Douglass, in his once-famous Fifth of July oration, delivered on July 5, 1852, could combine a militant rejection of slavery with a bow to the moral possibilities inherent in the Constitution to annihilate it—and this wasn't just a rhetorical gambit designed to win support for his cause: "In that instrument, I hold there is neither warrant, license, nor sanction of the hateful thing; but, interpreted as it ought to be interpreted, the Constitution is a GLORIOUS LIBERTY DOCUMENT. Read its preamble, consider its purposes. Is slavery among them? Is it at the gateway? or is it in the temple? It is neither." There is something glorious and, from a writerly point of view, beautiful in the truth that the document, which emancipated an entire slave class, comes to us first and weakly as a "proclamation" and only then permanently as a mere "amendment." Amendments are among the proper nouns of liberalism. This is the limited but real sense in which I mean to suggest that the first American Revolution was a success. In France, it took dictatorship, empire, revolution, and a failed coup before republican government could settle on a nearly acceptable constitution, and the liberal and republican face of the French revolution take precedence.

The American Revolution was violent, but its makers were ranged against vengeance. Thomas Paine, the most outspoken "leftist" of the American revolutionaries, was so respected as a kind of planetary radical, a "citizen of the world" in his own lovely phrase, that he was made a member of the National Assembly in France that condemned the king to death. Paine, however, spoke up defiantly and liberally, and at considerable personal risk, *against* the execution: "My language has always been that of liberty and humanity, and I know that nothing so exalts a nation as the union of these two principles. . . . What today seems an act of justice may then appear an act of vengeance. I had rather record a thousand errors on the side of mercy than be obliged to tell one act of severe justice." One cannot imagine even an in some ways humane Russian Bolshevik like Leon Trotsky, much less a bloody-minded French Jacobin like Robespierre, making a similar statement. Indeed, we know that Robespierre vehemently did not, rejecting any notion of mercy toward his perceived enemies: "To punish the oppressors of humanity is clemency; to forgive them is cruelty."

Or consider one of the best anecdotes of the American Revolution. It's the story of one Captain Asgill, who, as late as 1782, was sentenced by George Washington to be hanged in retaliation for an unpunished loyalist atrocity. Asgill had been chosen by lot as the victim. His mother, back home in London, wrote to the Count of Vergennes, the foreign minister of France, America's ally and Britain's adversary: "My son (and only Son) and dear as he is brave, amiable as deserving to be so . . . is now confined in America, an object of retaliation! Shall an innocent suffer for the guilty? Represent to yourself, Sir, the situation of a family under those circumstances; surrounded as I am by Objects of distress; distracted with fear & grief; no words can express my feelings or paint the scene." It worked. Vergennes forwarded the letter to Washington, and it became a cause célèbre in the new nation, exactly because of its call to a reciprocal humanity of suffering. "What must be the feelings of the many hundreds of . . . tender American mothers"—reading that letter—"whose sons in the early bloom of youth have perished in that sink of misery, the prison ship at New York?" one journalist wondered. Washington was glad to spare the boy, and a five-act tragedy was written in his honor in France.

Violence spilled over into vengeance often in the American Revolution, as the stories of the United Empire Loyalists, who built so much of my homeland of Canada, can testify. But revenge never became, as in so many other revolutions, including the French one, a perverse moral principle. To put it in the classical terms that Hamilton and Madison and Washington so loved and so often used, the liberals who made our revolution believed in the model of Cincinnatus rather than Caesar. Cincinnatus was the Roman general who retired to his farm; Caesar conquered and became a dictator. This pattern, of renouncing violence once its immediate ends are met, is deeply imprinted in the liberal temperament. It's why Grant and Eisenhower, victorious generals, took office in business suits (and often preferred other business-suited people to soldiers).

Liberals believe in fighting wars as hard as necessary; ending them as soon as possible; and rebuilding the defeated country as charitably as one can. The *necessity* of war making, including revolutionary war, is part of the liberal tradition: liberalism isn't pacifism and tries to learn the lesson of pacifist follies. But the cult and celebration of violence, including revolutionary violence for its own sake, is alien to the liberal way.

✿

The unforgivable sin of American slavery was imprinted in America's founding. But this historical fact, too, leads us to a basic liberal fact, or principle, even: liberalism seeks and eventually sees or admits its own failures. *Liberal reform, like evolutionary change, being incremental, is open to the evidence of experience.* Though humanism precedes modern science in the history of human thought—it was Galileo's father, a Renaissance lute player with a new system of tuning to promulgate, who introduced Galileo to the possibility of progressive empirical advance—it shares with it the readiness to search for the disconfirming instance.

And when reform has been essential, liberal democratic institutions have risen to the challenge. This has been true even when those institutions have been crippled by inequalities and injustices. Liberals have confidence in the possibility of reform, even when legislative institutions are very unequal and even undemocratic, because they understand that as long as formal freedoms are being respected, like the right of assembly and freedom of speech—values foreign to Montaigne but central to Hume and Smith and other liberals of their era—it's possible to put enormous stress on those institutions and force reforms even when they come reluctantly. The familiar critique of liberalism is that it depends too much on formal freedom; but actually, it is part of the shrewdness of liberalism to know that where formal freedom is defended, practical politics have to change. Social sympathy leads to improbable partnerships for decent causes.

So, yes, liberals believe in the *possibility* of reform. But liberals also believe in the *necessity* of reform. One of the things that distinguishes liberalism is the readiness to accept that social reform is *always* going to be essential. Each time we alter a society, new inequalities and injustices appear and are in need of remedy. The civil rights movement triumphs in its immediate objectives, if not its long-term goals, but even its limited success reminds us that women's freedom is hardly fully achieved. And as women's freedom is achieved, we ask about sexual minorities, and so on.

The left's reproach to this view is that reform is never enough; the right's reproach is that reform is never finished. The hardened liberal can never make up her mind which is the most beautiful word in the language, *compulsory* or *forbidden*. Indeed, it is the compulsive appetite for reform that makes conservatives laugh at liberals, and ought to make liberals laugh at themselves from time to time. Reform our language, our pronouns, our cafeteria menus, our forms of addressing each other. Reform sexual acts so that they demand step-by-step consent. Some of this *is* ridiculous or can be ridiculously enforced.

But our experience shows that reform *is* almost always necessary. On the whole, the reformers have got it right, even when no one thought they had. It is hard to recall how many even reasonable-seeming people thought slavery was tolerable. Or what a subject for laughter votes for women once was. Or how easily self-approving conservatives like William Buckley were perfectly content with perpetuating apartheid in the American South. For that matter, we only need look at the fight for marriage equality to recall how recently even liberal-minded people were suspicious of gay marriage. Now, the remaining arguments, except among hard-core resistors, are about how we fold gay marriage into a larger social blend. We may or may not be indignant about the refusal of a baker to make a cake for a gay wedding—but that we are arguing about this is in itself proof of how acceptable marriage between people of the same sex has become.

All reform, *always*? This seems implausible, surely? The secret truth is that what we are having most of the time is the *same* reform, over and over again, directed to new places and people: a removal of socially sanctioned cruelty. Montaigne's insistence on compassion, like Smith and Hume's on sympathy, points to a permanent feature of our social natures. Cruelty happens; sympathy cures it. The next reform is necessary not because we changed our views but because new kinds of cruelty are always coming into existence or into view. Our sight sharpens. Our circles of compassion enlarge. No sane society reaches a secure balance point. We always need change. The process of reform is never ending not because we are always searching for utopia but because as the growth of knowledge alters our conditions, we need new understandings to change our plans.

Finally, liberal reform drives toward *egalitarian* ends— ones in which equality of opportunity is evidenced by equality of outcome. We know a race is fair when the same people don't always win it. Many conservatives want their world to be peaceful, prosperous, and pluralist, just as liberals do, but they don't particularly care that it be *fair*. They traditionally shrug at inequality among the few, if a general happiness is widely dispersed among many. This doesn't mean that they were all mere footmen to the powerful. Dr. Johnson and Benjamin Disraeli, both from unprivileged backgrounds, felt this way. They weren't trying to please their superiors; they were saying what they thought they saw: a society seemed to function best with an elite caste at the top overseeing a benevolent order below. Both were content *not* to belong to the governing caste and accept the benefits of its existence. Dr. Johnson says better that some be unhappy than that all be equally miserable.

But liberals believe that reducing social distances is an inherent good because a society can't be truly pluralist if it is class divided. There's a wonderful moment in Charles Dickens's *Hard Times* that sums up the point perfectly. A visiting Utilitarian school supervisor demands of a poor girl, "Girl number twenty, isn't this a prosperous nation, and a'n't you in a thriving state?" She wisely confesses that she "couldn't know whether it was a prosperous nation or not, and whether I was in a thriving state or not, unless I knew who had got the money, and whether any of it was mine."

But how does liberal reform happen? Mill and Taylor and their circle insisted that reform was possible even within inequitable institutions and that a virtuous circle could begin even in the face of gross unfairness: change an institution in small measures and it will eventually improve in larger ones. Small loopholes in the oligarchy—which, for instance, allowed some metropolitan seats in British Parliament to be recognizably more representative than others—could be seized on and exploited. The genuinely altruistic instincts and far-sighted insights of some on the Whig side of the oligarchy in power could be courted: Anthony Trollope's political novels are a long dramatization of the story of that courtship of Whigs by liberals and how it happened. Spurred on certainly by public demonstrations in parks and parade grounds—another subject in our foundational liberal sentence—both the educated classes and the working classes who were fighting for reform in mid-nineteenth-century Britain did not abandon their commitment to those essential dance steps of nonviolent tactics, constitutional means, and democratic procedures.

One of the most important empirical truths of the past centuries has been that the lack of something even approaching perfect democracy has not been a barrier to effective change when a country becomes ready for it. The British Parliament in the nineteenth century was a kind of family compact among gentlemen, but by the end of the century radical social change had taken place within it, including a broadly if imperfectly expanded right to vote. It had altered itself under the pressure of circumstances. The path of liberal activism was well described, with typical tartness, by Trollope, who put the formula into the mouth of his radical politician, Mr. Monk: "Many who before regarded legislation on the subject as chimerical, will now fancy that it is only dangerous, or perhaps not more than difficult. And so, in time it will come to be looked on as among the things possible, then among the things probable;—and so at last it will be ranged in the list of those few measures which the country requires as being absolutely needed. That is the way in which public opinion is made." The movement for gay marriage in America, if someone could write its history properly, is almost a textbook case of Trollope's idea of how political reform happens at its best: an impossible idea becomes possible, then becomes necessary, and then all but a minority—a strenuous minority, often—accept its inevitability. The job of those trying to make change happen is not to hector it into the agenda of the necessary but to move it into the realm of the plausible—and once something is plausible, even in a semidemocratic society, it has a natural momentum toward becoming real.

Trollope believed in this model while recognizing that much of the power was still held in the British Parliament by an oligarchy even more limited than our own. He put the liberal positon very early and well and from the other end of Victorian society. In a letter to R. Dudley Baxter, an English economist, he wrote: "Liberals think it to be for the welfare of the people and the good of the country that distances should be reduced and gradually annihilated." "Gradually annihilated"—it's a stronger term than it may seem. Distances can be *annihilated*, not just reduced, though often only slowly. The American Congress is now, and has always been, crippled by the power of big money and brutally antidemocratic traditions, including the existence of a Senate that gives tiny rural states power equal to big urban ones. But big reforms have happened all the same—though not without conflict, backsliding, difficulty, and even violence. Still, working-class people and women have the vote, African Americans have civil rights, speech is more or less free—the "mere" reformist project has worked, again and again.

Almost invariably, what happens when a radical reform is achieved by democratic means is that we no longer experience it as radical. The Labour Party in Britain for instance, just after the Second World War, took on itself the task of nationalizing a large part of the hitherto free market—yet did it entirely within the framework of the kind of openly debated reform that is the hallmark of the liberal tradition. It was, in every sense, a reform both radical and liberal, the latter even though it involved curbing free-market practices. Many people—some, like Friedrich Hayek, serious and in many respects admirable thinkers about man and state, emboldened by the rise of totalitarianism to question the social-democratic consensus they saw rising around them— were sure that this could only mark an end to larger civic freedoms. But Hayek could not have been more wrong, as he himself was eventually prepared to admit. The reforms brought in may or may not have all been successful. But no significant civil liberty was even remotely threatened, while the method and manner in which the reforms were achieved left them open to further debate and further reform, including free-market reform. It was a triumph of the liberal system of institutionalized argument.

So, liberal activism is distinct, historically and intellectually, from left activism. They begin with different premises and end in different orders. The left in America today sees gerrymandering, corporate lobbying, and political funding—the obscene truth that more money buys more speech— and even the existence of the electoral college as signs of a fundamentally corrupt system that is not worth saving. Liberals, however, say that these things are lamentable, difficult, and desperately in need of reform and still think that reform *can* happen, given a passionately purposeful commitment to liberal institutions. In the mid-nineteenth century, the fight for the enfranchisement of the working classes was as high a mountain as reform could hope to scale; less than one long lifetime later, Clement Attlee's first Labour cabinet had in it seven men who had begun their lives as coal miners. Where we are now, in terms of democratic deficits, may not at first look better than it was twenty years ago. But it is incomparably better than it was a hundred years ago.

⚜

Yet instead of simply emphasizing parliamentary or government action alone—reform through legislative and executive action or even political action as the goal of liberalism—our awkward rhino, our liberal sentence, spoke of "unimpeded conversation, demonstration, and debate," a very different and, at first, much squishier thing. Why is that? It's obvious that liberalism depends on democratic institutions: parliaments in Britain and Canada and India, state and federal legislatures and courts in the United States. The story of liberalism is in part the story of how those institutions got broadened by ever more universal suffrage. But it also depends on communities and changes that take place *outside* political institutions. The real source of reform is often far from any obvious political action. Morals and manners change politics more than politics change morals and manners.

No couple could represent the memorable moment in the 1860s when that idea began to blossom into an encompassing theater of action—into a real liberal revolution of acting and thinking and building—than the pair at the center of another great liberal love story of the Victorian age: George Henry Lewes and Marian Evans, whom we know better as the novelist George Eliot. Just as passionate and, if anything, even more courageous than Taylor and Mill, actually living as a married couple without benefit of clergy, they represent the emerging and more practical-potent liberalism of the 1850s and 1860s as Taylor and Mill embodied the idealism of the 1830s and 1840s. Lewes was a direct protégé of Mill's and together with Eliot helped press liberalism into a deeper dialogue with science and systems, in ways that are prophetic about the insights into community and change that we are learning about again today. Where Taylor and Mill were liberals of *principle*, Lewes and Eliot were liberals of *process*. Taylor and Mill wanted to articulate new ideals of progress; Lewes and Eliot, as Darwinians, wanted to understand how change happens in complex systems.

Eliot was, with her friends Trollope and Charles Dickens, one of the three greatest novelists of the greatest period in the English novel. (Thackeray, who would have formed a fourth in their own time, has tended to fall away since.) Lewes, though much less known, was the most important and scintillating and above all loveable English-language liberal journalist of his day. He was an amazing polymath, equally expert—which means, as every supposed polymath knows, in some ways equally inexpert—at everything from microscopy to the life of Goethe. He ran the leading London liberal journal of the 1850s, *The Leader*, which came as close to summing up what liberalism is as any journal can. Each issue bore the same perfectly chosen liberal epigraph—awkwardly written, as we've learned that liberal epigraphs are—from Wilhelm von Humboldt, the same German thinker who had given Mill the idea of self-development: "The one idea which History exhibits as evermore developing itself into greater distinctness is the Idea of Humanity—the noble endeavor to throw down all the barriers erected between men by prejudice and one-sided views, and by setting aside the distinctions of Religion, Country and Color, to treat the whole Human race as one brotherhood."

Lewes could say something smart about any subject under the sun. He wrote brilliantly about acting and actors; stagestruck, he was perhaps the first actor on the English-speaking stage to attempt a wholly sympathetic Shylock. His writing on theater is the best in English between Hazlitt and Shaw. His book on actors and acting even contains what is still the most concise epigraphic description of the actor's art: "The selection of idealized expressions which shall, to the spectator, be symbols of real emotion." He was the complete liberal thinker of the nineteenth century. To see in this immensely social and utterly altruistic-minded man—who was ready to claim his wife's lovers' children as his own for the sake of domestic peace— the self-seeking individualist liberal of the orthodox clichés is not to see G. H. Lewes as he was.

But all of it would be forgotten if not for the greatest act of Lewes life, which was, if not self-abasing, then certainly self-subsuming: he became the support and mentor and lover of Marian Evans. The story of Lewes and Evans's romance is still startling given our prejudices and expectations about Victorian propriety. Lewes had, in 1853, when he began his love affair with Evans, long been married to another woman, who, bizarrely, had been living more or less openly with another man—in the same house with Lewes, much like the Taylor-Mills arrangement. (That man was Thornton Hunt, the son of Leigh Hunt, the great friend of Shelley, whom Dickens caricatured as Harold Skimpole in *Bleak House*). The complexities of this meant that Lewes—having generously claimed fathership for a child not his own—was now prevented by his own claim from getting divorced.

George and Marian fell in love at once. He was ugly, she was plain; he was outgoing, she was shy. She was, though, possessed of a line of calm courage that would be the making of her moral life; at only twenty-two she had announced to her father that she no longer accepted Christianity and had nearly been booted out of the house. Yet they instantly spied in each the one right soulmate—their own word—and with enormous brio and self-condolence for two not terribly brazen people, living very much within the constraints of London society, albeit its more Bohemian edge, they simply declared themselves married, the world be damned. Marian wrote to her brother Isaac that she was now Mrs. Lewes, and he wrote back, with crushing asperity, demanding to know where the ceremony had taken place. She replied that there had been no ceremony; they were simply married.

Lewes was a smart man, but the smartest thing he ever did was to recognize that Evans was far more gifted than he was. He recognized her genius, insisted that she write fiction, and she was not very long after launched into the success, artistic and commercial, of *Adam Bede*. She always recognized how vital his impetus had been, even taking the name George in tribute to his love. (Eliot was either a simple flat appendage, or perhaps a pun on his initials.)

A kind of conversation went on between Lewes's ideas about politics and her far superior instincts for art. I say instincts, but in fact she was, of those three greatest English Victorian novelists, very much the most intellectual. Trollope was a limitlessly shrewd practical observer of parliamentary life and of community politics; Dickens was a great instinctive poet and myth maker, though with often confused political ideas. (When the "Jamaica committees" were formed to protest British maltreatment of rebels during a colonial revolt, Dickens sided with the soldiers.) Eliot, with Lewes, was a true intellectual, someone who lived by and with ideas.

This made her politics specific but peculiar. She was a feminist, but of a very particular kind. She was, a little shockingly, *against* women's suffrage when Mill, then an M.P., proposed it, quixotically, in Parliament. It wasn't that she thought women's suffrage wrong, exactly, but that in another sense, more prescient of our current preoccupations, she saw that political freedom would never be enough. If freedom wasn't rooted in women being able to claim their private lives for themselves, they didn't have it. Freedom begins in the bedroom and in the mind. That was why she was, for all her hesitation about suffrage, unimpeded in her enthusiasm for women's education and pressed for the establishment of a women's college at Cambridge.

The belief that liberation begins in the bedroom, that women have to feel free at home before they can be free in the world, was one lesson of Dorothea's marriage to Mr. Casaubon in *Middlemarch*, the at-first impressive and soon-enough puerile pedant who is writing his fatuous "Key to All Mythologies." Dorothea's enslavement to a lesser mind domestically is like the enslavement of all women to a lesser place politically. It was an extension of Harriet Taylor's observation about the little dictator at the dinner table, with the additional truth that too many women choose their own dictator from mistaken infatuation, repented over a lifetime. (Many identified Lewes as Casaubon, quite wrongly, as she insisted. His problem was just the opposite of Casaubon's, not an inability to finish but an incapacity for extended focus.)

Lewes began as a classical positive liberal, under the direct influence of Mill. He believed in reform as a series of legislative measures. But under the press of his perpetual dialogue with his wife, he moved deeper. Together they began to embrace a Darwinian liberalism, one that included, instinctively, insights about the anchorage of liberalism in small alterations that would take another century to systematize.

Their ideas—that formal freedom is not enough, that the private is political, that changes made in many small lives can become the ground for genuine emancipation—can take an inward or outward turn. One of the things that makes *Middlemarch* a great book is that Dorothea, the heroine, learns to distinguish between her seeming upward ascension to intellect through her enslavement to Casaubon, the wrong husband, before finding herself in a more honest "sideways" relationship with a better, reform-minded partner, Ladislaw, sort of a moodier provincial Lewes. She remains bound, but not chained, to a domestic role.

The influence of Eliot on Lewes was just as great as his on her. All the things that supportive wives are traditionally expected to do for creative husbands, he did for her. He protected her from mean criticism, read her first drafts, and listened to her middle-of-the-night letters to editors and uncomprehending critics. He was the wind beneath her wings, the force behind her forcefulness. But together they moved into a particular new kind of empiricism: in a lovely phrase she said she wanted to "escape from all vagueness and inaccuracy into the daylight of distinct vivid ideas." In place of his early journalistic, swashbuckling liberalism, polemical and self-delighted, Lewes became a patiently empirical liberal. He was determined to see things as they are in order to make them better. He saw that science proceeded not from the accumulation of facts but from a readiness to be surprised. "We must resolve that when we ask Nature a question, to listen patiently to her reply; should that reply perplex us, we must ask again, putting the question in another form; and should again, and again, the same reply be elicited, we must accept it, be it ever so destructive of our theories and anticipations."

He also became aware in a very prescient way, which would not be commonplace for another hundred years, of the common origins of art, novel writing, and the sciences, particularly biology, in leaps of the imagination that sweep beyond the facts at hand. And as a consequence, his new form of liberalism became a new model: the latter part of his career is just as committed to reform but is one committed out of observed particulars.

Lewes and Eliot between them, someone has said, a little pretentiously but not wrongly, defined the liberalism of the *oikos*, the Greek word for home, whereas Trollope's is the liberalism of the *polis*, the city. Lewes and Eliot were more prescient of our own preoccupations: reform had to pass through the living room before it could move to Parliament. The will to go deep into a society, or a physical system, to see what made it tick made them see themselves, by the 1860s, as engaged in a liberalism less flamboyant, more foundational than that of the Mill and Taylor generation.

What I mean when I say that Lewes and Eliot represented "liberals of process" may become more tangible—even smelly—if we think about one of the greatest liberal reforms of their time: the creation of the London sewers. London had been caught for a century in a "miasma of raw sewage, which was rightly believed to be a public health threat, though wrongly, in the years before bacterial theories of disease were fully understood, thought to enter our bodies through a kind of malignant fog. The work of making a safer sewer took two generations and many efforts. Lewes was a close observer of this process. He was intimate friends with F. O. Ward, "the man of the Sewers" and the sanitary affairs writer for the *London Times*, who even invented a new kind of water closet. (He closely studied the sewage system of Brussels to find the right model, and there was much intense argument about mixing waste and rainwater.) The new system was eventually brought in as the result of the Great Stink of 1858. It took a long time to finish building, but it saved—by direct protection from cholera in London and by indirect example to other cities—hundreds of thousands and, in the long term, possibly millions of lives. Remaking the London sewers required a process of reasoned reform—not merely good principle but evidence and argument and engineering, all unfolding not in a eureka moment in Parliament but over decades of effort underground. The principle of public good and the process of public works became the same.

That's what we mean by "liberals of process." We mean that where the Mill generation were obsessed with how individuals could be freed from common prejudices, the Lewes generation were concerned, in a manner that derives from

Darwin, with how individuals change as their environments alter. The complex *process* of building public sanitation was inseparable from the abstract *principle* of the public good. People made pipes, and pipes made better people. The sewer was the sanity.

But it wasn't all sewers and moral support for Lewes. He was also the first to use a term, and discover a concept, that remains one of the key analytic weapons in the liberal arsenal. This was the idea of "emergence"—the great solvent of all determinisms. Lewes's discovery of emergence was simply the discovery that the rules of a system can be completely different than the rules of the elements that form it. Hydrogen and oxygen make water, but water is not like either. Atoms alone form molecules, but the laws of thermodynamics are completely different from the laws of quantum electrodynamics. Systems are made up of their parts, but the parts are not the system. As Lewes wrote: "The emergent is unlike its components insofar as these are incommensurable, and it cannot be reduced to their sum or their difference."

In a way, Lewes's idea was simply a more sweeping statement of the same principle that Hume and Smith had offered: they saw that acts of buying and selling could arise from sympathy as much as greed and end in some place larger than a store—that they could help make a city. The market, like any other system, has emergent properties of its own and creates structures it never planned. In Greenwich Village in the 1950s, the small businesspeople, the locksmiths, bread bakers, and shoe repairmen—who are there simply to sell goods and services—become a network, carrying civic functions of connecting, protecting, observing, communing. This beautiful "ballet of the street" is what the great urbanist Jane Jacobs loved to celebrate; it's an instance of an emergent system, right on the sidewalk. (And of course, the system can turn on us and produce a monoculture of bank branches and chain drugstores that destroys, and renders robotic, the original ballet.)

Autocracies and authoritarians of all stripes want to reduce all things to their elements: we are no more than the race or class or kind we come from. Lewes was saying that the systems that we live in can become very different from the elements they began with even if no one element in that system wills it, or even alters its nature. The system emerging is more important than the elements originally engaged. The origins of our systems, and of our ideas, are less important than the ideas themselves. Slave holders can write documents that carry within them the necessity of the annihilation of slavery.

Eliot said the same things in her books, which are often arguments about how original elements—a British Jew or a lonely woman—can become more than they thought they could when swimming in a new system. The literary critic Phillip Davis has beautifully traced the ways in which Lewes's ideas on emergence, which Eliot had often edited and improved, are present in her fiction as permanent patterns of human behavior: "Lewes's microscopic process transferred to the study of human beings." Eliot came to understand, and study, the ways in which the endless minutiae of social life are the real ground of our behavior, and the slow but willed transitions between social roles—girl to wife, wife to mother, wife and mother to liberated woman—the truth of our existence. That *all* behavior is emergent was their coauthored lesson.

Throughout Eliot's novels, and particularly in *Middlemarch*, the social roles people are assigned turn out to be mutable—never fatalistic in their doom, as in Thomas Hardy, and capable of alteration without being attached to a romantic idea of overt rebellion. Against Dickens's beautiful and perfectly etched series of tics and mannerisms, Eliot watches people change, from year to year and even from week to week. Dorothea and Casaubon find within a few days that their marriage is not the coloration of minds that she at least had imagined but a bondage in folly. In *Adam Bede*, Arthur Donnithorne becomes a liar not through some inner trauma but by following the logic of his actions. "There is a terrible coercion in our deeds, which may first turn the honest man into a deceiver and then reconcile him to the change, for this reason—that the second wrong presents itself to him in the guise of the only practicable right." What happens in her fiction is always emergent, not resultant, and depends on slow processes that suddenly make people leap out into new and unseen states. As she wrote in *Middlemarch*, she wanted to "pierce the obscurity of those minute processes which prepare human misery and joy, those invisible thoroughfares which are the first lurking places of anguish, mania, and crime, that delicate poise and transition which determine the growth of happy or unhappy consciousness." The unpredictable complexity of causes was clear to Eliot in her novels—but so was the eternal possibility of change.

Lewes died of enteritis—though it may have been colon cancer—in 1878, and, a nice ironic capper on their story,

scarcely two years later Marian married John Cross, an admirer twenty years younger than herself, a proper marriage
in a proper church. Many people were as scandalized by
her second swift marriage as they had been by her first im-
provised one. But she insisted, and all the evidence suggests
rightly, that it was just what Lewes would have wanted. Her
second marriage lasted, sadly, only seven months. She died
of kidney disease on December 22, 1880, and, like Harriet
Taylor, was buried alongside her first soulmate. He had emboldened her. He had taught her, liberally—they had taught
each other—to seize the day, to be unafraid of popular opinion, to find in love not passion alone but the best kind of
sense there is, the redemptive sense of the particular occasion, life seen in the daylight of the distinctive.

✥

George Eliot's "invisible thoroughfares," the buried tracks of
common emotion, remain the pathways of liberal reform.
The reason liberals are confident that reform can happen is
because they know, instinctively and empirically, that much
of the work of reform is largely done before politics take
place. One of the things that we have genuinely learned is
that the existence of invisible thoroughfares of voluntary
and unplanned and private arenas of argument and debate
are essential preconditions for liberal societies. Once again,
humanism precedes liberalism.

Two contemporary thinkers have helped systematize
and renew this insight, though they may not always spring
to mind as liberal philosophers: the Harvard political scientist Robert Putnam and the German philosopher Jürgen

Habermas. Putnam became famous in the nineties for his book *Bowling Alone: The Collapse and Revival of American Community*, which was taken, not entirely wrongly, as a plea against the stripped-down communal life of America in the age of the automobile and mall. But the real importance and value of his work lies in his studies of what makes democracies happen—the most famous being his examination of the decentralized "devolved" government in Italy. He spent years studying what happened when the powerful central government of Italy in Rome democratized itself and offered local power.

What makes local democratic government more or less satisfactory, more or less honest, more or less effective? What Putnam discovered is that intermediate institutions—intermediate between individuals and the state—made the crucial difference. In plain English—or at least in translated Italian—if there were a lot of amateur opera groups around, then democratic institutions were more likely to flourish and work better. In Northern Italy, where citizens participate actively in sports clubs, literary guilds, service groups, and choral societies, regional governments are, Putnam said, "efficient in their internal operation, creative in their policy initiatives and effective in implementing those initiatives." In Southern Italy, by contrast, where patterns of civic engagement are far weaker, regional governments tend to be corrupt and inefficient.

Putnam used the term *social capital* to characterize the relationship between "strong networks of citizen participation and positive institutional performance." Carles Boix and Daniel Posner defined this term, in their review of his book *Making Democracy Work*, as "the networks, norms of reciprocity and trust that are fostered among the members of community associations by virtue of their experience of social interaction and cooperation." Mere proximity counts for a lot. Learning to live and work in peace with other people with whom you don't share genes or a creed is the foundation of modern freedom.

Liberal institutions, including freedom of faith, allow social capital to accumulate, even in times of political frustration. The black church in the South was the crucial and long-standing repository of social capital for the civil rights movement. Indeed, it wouldn't be far off to say that the black churches, throughout the near century of terror-enforced apartheid in the South, were accumulating sufficient social capital—networks of alliances and ideals and mutual solidarities, along with the general admiration of even those outside it; no one could pretend that the black preachers were not admirable people—that eventually they could "cash in" as a movement for radical social change.

Jürgen Habermas is the German philosopher who anticipated Putnam's insight, in talking about what he called the "primacy of the public sphere"—both historically, in the evolution of liberal institutions, and by extension practically, in asking what makes them work now. The coffeehouses and salons of the seventeenth and eighteenth centuries, he argued, helped provide the foundation of the liberal Enlightenment—a caffeinated pathway out of clan society into cosmopolitan society. Democracy was not made in the streets but among the saucers. He showed not only that clubs and coffeehouses precede parliaments, but that a parliament can only be as strong as the coffeehouse beside it. (This isn't just a *mot*. Everyone in Paris still knows and can point out the cafés where members of the National Assembly go before and between sessions—where the real work gets done.) When social spaces begin to be created outside the direct control of the state (including commercial ones, run for profit), civil society can start to flourish in unexpected ways. Learning just to sip alongside a stranger makes for a potable kind of pluralism.

Isn't the presence of this public sphere self-evident? Well—to use the essential liberal answer—yes and no. Every thinker only makes sense if you can understand his particular problem situation, and Habermas was presented with as acute a situation as anyone could find. His father was a Nazi sympathizer, and he grew up in the catastrophe of the war. He trained with the Frankfurt school and found their Marxist analysis intriguing but ultimately too determinist. Was there a way to think about rational communication among people that didn't depend on believing that the cosmos was itself rational or that people in some sense always were? Habermas's answer was that the world might not be reasonable, and people certainly weren't, but that public spaces could help them become so. Habermas tells us that the "public sphere . . . which mediates between society and state" is the place "in which the public organizes itself as the bearer of public opinion." A bit Germanic in tone, what he means is simply that what Putnam showed to be true in today's Italy had also been true in eighteenth-century Europe. Webs of social development appeared in cities—in theaters, museums, meeting rooms, opera houses—and those centers of sociability became the crucible of change. The American sociologist Howie Becker back in the 1940s arrived at a similar conclusion. He came to what he calls the "long crawl" theory of social worlds after the endless crawls or credits that appear at the end of movies, some of which become classics. All of those people made *The Wizard of Oz* or *Singin' in the Rain.* No one single person needs to be a genius or a visionary or even a great artist for the result to be permanent and to transcend generations. In the same way, the clubs we make are collectively smarter than the people we are. Reason, like musicals, emerges from the meeting of many minds.

The most poetic term to describe the public sphere or social capital comes from Frederick Law Olmsted, the designer of Central Park. Olmsted, though most famous now as a kind of urban pastoralist, was one of the first great American journalists whose series of reports on slavery in the pre–Civil War South constituted one of the first hits the *New York Times* (then the *New York Daily Times*) ever published. Olmsted, comparing the southern states with the North, saw that, for all of its cultural self-proclamation, the South was a paralyzed, frozen society, while the North was full of activity: "our young men . . . are members and managers of reading-rooms, public libraries, gymnasiums, game-clubs, boat-clubs, ball-clubs, and all sorts of clubs, Bible classes, debating-societies, military companies; they are planting road-side trees, or damming streams for skating-ponds, or rigging diving-boards, or getting up fireworks displays, or private theatricals; they are always doing something." This is Putnam's idea, a hundred and fifty years early. Olmsted even called this orgy of sociability by a beautiful name—commonplace civilization.

In many ways, this is the cumulative understanding of liberalism. It touches on compassion, sympathy, community, emergent states, and decent coffee. One could almost join these terms up into a single progressive equation: social capital made by small communities produces the public sphere, whose debates create our commonplace civilization. They clear the ground or the field in which liberal societies can grow. That these beliefs in social capital and commonplace civilization have been at the heart of liberal thought from its earliest modern beginnings is easily missed, but essential.

⁂

OK, I can hear you say, Olivia, I get it. Montaigne was a sweet guy, social sympathy is a positive thing, cafés count for a lot—it's why I do all my homework at the Starbucks—and sure the Leweses sound like a great couple. But what does this have to do with our life now? What we're facing today is so much more insidious and far-reaching. You can't think that all that patient liberal incrementalism can still work in the face of state-sanctioned cruelty of the magnitude we're witnessing today, can you?

If all these thoughts on common sympathy and the public sphere, on studying systems and changing small orders, seem too abstract, too rooted in things and people that happened in the eighteenth and nineteenth centuries, let me try and show you their relevance to the most startling and least talked about of all public developments in America in the past half century: the great crime decline.

Violent crime, which was a plague that shaped—and deformed—American public argument for decades, suddenly and precipitously began to decline in the early 1990s and has continued declining ever since, reshaping the civic order. In

New York City alone, where, as the sociologist Patrick Shar- key has written, "more than 2,000 people used to be mur- dered each year, 328 were killed in 2014, the lowest number since the first half of the twentieth century." (Each year, the number keeps dropping.) It isn't just New York. Violent crime fell in Atlanta, Dallas, Los Angeles, and Washington, and not by a little but by a lot. More important, the quality of life changed dramatically, particularly for the most vul- nerable. In Cleveland in the eighties, the level of violence in poor neighborhoods was about 70 percent higher than in the rest of the city; by 2010, that number had dropped to 24 percent. The inner city was revived from Portland, Maine, to Portland, Oregon. It is the most astonishing alteration in urban life in the century.

But, by the usual rule that we see bad news more clearly than good, this miracle has been largely overlooked. In- stead, ironically, the results of lower crime, particularly the repeopling of cities by the affluent, are now seen as new social problems. (Liberals know that, when we solve a social problem, what we most often see is the *new* social problem that the solution creates.) The causes of this miracle, though, mirror the insights of all those novelists and essayists and sociologists and philosophers and historians about how the liberalism of shared values and communities can rescue it- self when it falls into crisis. An argument used to be made that mass incarceration played a role in the decline, in re- moving those who committed violent acts from society. But any close study of the facts shows that this played, at most, a minor role, and in any case, as incarceration decreases, crime continues to go down. The claim that the aggressive stop-and-frisk of minorities in particular was responsible has also been refuted; the practice, far from uniformly executed in any case, was curtailed, and crime continues to disappear.

Today, sociologists have made a very compelling case that community policing, married to community action, is the real engine behind the crime decline. Community groups (the Habermasian coffeehouses in this case) began policing their own neighborhoods, and police became more aware of the community pressure points, stopping crime where it started before it happened and using predictive data more efficiently. What the police did that *really* mattered was to get to the scene of the crime before crime could happen. Above all, as Sharkey has said, "[The crime decline] happened because city spaces transformed. After years in which urban neighborhoods were largely abandoned, left on their own, a whole bunch of different actors came together and transformed [them]."

So the primacy of the public sphere isn't just an abstraction of a German philosopher dreaming of a French café. It's what stopped crime in the South Bronx. The power of emergent systems, positive circles of change, isn't just a nineteenth-century idea. It's a living truth. It wasn't that the neighborhoods in the South Bronx were magically altered. It was that the world changed around them, and they changed with their world. The social order of the South Bronx, it turned out, couldn't be reduced to fixed unchanging elements that had to be either profoundly altered or abandoned. Conservatives, and leftists too, insisted that only if we made fundamental, foundational change could we hope to affect violent crime. We had to fix the "broken black family" or else end inequality.

No, we didn't. As people made small incremental changes in their neighborhoods, virtuous circles of sympathy emerged—because the subways seemed safer, more people rode the trains, making the subway safer still—and the entire social system changed. Violent crime, against every expectation, effectively disappeared, as a safer social system of order emerged around it. Process liberalism worked.

Like any appealing term, *social capital* and the *public sphere* and even *commonplace civilization* risk becoming mere catchall phrases. Plenty of time can be spent criticizing them as bland evasions of real political conflict. After all, the difference between Northern and Southern Italy isn't just happy amateur opera singers versus gloomy suspicious men under the spell of *omerta*. The differences in economic possibility, in feudal agriculture and criminality and industrialization, play a part. Similarly, the North didn't win the Civil War only, or even chiefly, because northern cities had more fireworks displays. The North won because it turned fireworks into gunpowder and then fired the guns and built the trains and hired the generals willing to use them in indiscrete mass killings.

But a catchall phrase does catch something, and I don't think we can doubt that these catch much. Humanism precedes liberalism. Connection comes before action. A readiness for self-inspection precedes an effort at self-improvement, and a confidence in our neighbors precedes faith in citizenship. Thinking about liberal order or the liberal future in terms of laws and legislatures is far too limiting. Park designers, sociologists, and beyond have more to tell us about building open societies.

The liberal idea of community is not the traditional one. Where conservatives believe in the renewal of traditional community, liberals believe as well in the flight *from* family and tradition into new kinds of communal order, which is why utopian communities and, for that matter, Bohemian neighborhoods have played such a large role in liberal history. (We can't imagine American liberalism without imagining Greenwich Village.) The conservative idea of community is a way of preserving tradition; the liberal idea of community is one of assembling confidence and energies for reform. Building social capital, or civic society, is a way of having self-government outside government, not just a way of reaffirming familiar values. On the contrary, the values it affirms are usually rebellious: the possibility of abolition or free thinking or feminism or, in the social capital of the black church, equal rights.

And while liberals accept that manners make morals, they ought to be indignant when even the most constitutional-minded conservatives point to manners as though these alone were enough to make social movements. The civil rights movement certainly grew out of the social capital of the black church. But it cashed that capital into law. The crime decline certainly was rooted in retaking neighborhoods, block by block. But that civic enterprise had to be reinforced by city politics. A belief in the importance of community and family and small measures is worthless if it is only a cocoon for the comfortable. Olmsted, believing that slavery crippled commonplace civilization, thought that was one of the reasons slavery had to end. Commonplace civilization has to be the catapult of activism, not a refuge from it.

Return to our awkward liberal sentence. Why "demonstration" and why "mostly unimpeded"? I mean of course *demonstration* in the broadest sense—nonviolent social action that moves a discussion from the coffeehouse to the avenue. In our day, these include social media storms and YouTube protest videos and, occasionally, cable television programming at night.

But I also mean demonstration in the very literal sense that became familiar in the sixties and continues today: large numbers of people taking to the streets in nonviolent protests to show the depth of their desire for reform. Demonstrations can seem impotent and old fashioned. Any footsore liberal who has gone on a lot of these marches will be doubtful about their efficacy; but, truth be told, demonstrations have been hugely efficient means of conducting a conversation into a political project, whether it's the Chartist march in Britain in the 1830s or the March on Washington for Jobs and Freedom in 1963.

And, indeed, thinking about the power of public demonstration makes me want you to meet one last liberal, still insufficiently appreciated, one who embodies all the liberal virtues *as* action, *in* action. That liberal is Bayard Rustin, the guy who enumerated those three vital dance steps. Rustin was a gay man and about as open as one could be in the early postwar era. He walked a tightrope: black and gay, socialist and liberal, committed to nonviolence and diversity of coalition at a time when black anger propelled many of those closest to him toward their own form of racial nationalism. He was arrested more than twenty-five times and remained elegant throughout, which made him all the more enraging to his persecutors. He was arrested for civil rights activism and on at least one morals charge, which cost him sixty days in a jail in Los Angeles County and shocked his allies on the progressive side, who saw homosexuality as an "agony" at worst and a "problem" at best—much as his enemies did.

Born in Pennsylvania, raised by a Quaker grandmother, he eventually turned himself into a model of gay stylishness in New York City. (He was an obsessive shopper for beautiful things at flea markets, making him dear to my heart.) But he had been converted to Gandhian nonviolence as a young man, and few were more devout practitioners of that hyperdemanding ethical practice. He went to prison in the forties because he conscientiously objected to the draft, and though one might question his judgment in the case of the war against the Nazis, no one can question his courage. He endured the worst kinds of privations in brutal imprisonment—as he would do again and again throughout his life—not only with stoicism but with enormous humanity. You won't find many more moving documents in American literature than the letters he wrote to wardens and even "gang bosses." At one point he was arrested for participating in a civil rights struggle and put on a chain gang, but he still managed to recognize the humanity of the wardens and thereby insisted, through his letters, that they treat him humanely too. (These letters were more successful than one might imagine.)

He became a protégé of A. Philip Randolph—the founder of the first powerful African American union, the Brotherhood of Sleeping Car Porters, and a pioneer among the first generation of civil rights leaders—at a time when racism and apartheid were still uncritically accepted by even well-meaning Americans. And so, the struggle for economic justice alongside racial justice became foundational for Rustin, as was the absolute necessity for coalition and compromise. He was a union guy for both practical reasons (unions were still the basis then of liberal politics) and ethical ones (he took the union organizers' lesson that ethnic politics always had to be entangled with economic ones to heart). He was always very clear headed, in ways that not everyone around him was, on the basic arithmetic of the American civil rights struggle, understanding that with African Americans scarcely constituting 10 percent of the population they could only function with allies in white America.

He was introduced to Dr. King in the fifties, and it's no exaggeration to say that Rustin taught King the rudiments and then the rules of nonviolent protest and resistance that would propel the civil rights struggle. King was a kind of astonishing prodigy of protest. He had organized the Montgomery boycott more or less instinctively and had been thrust into a position of leadership because of his gifts as an orator. But like many other speakers and leaders, he had to improvise his own ideology, hearing what he and others say.

King broke with Rustin in the early sixties in the ugliest possible way. Adam Clayton Powell—a not terribly admirable but very powerful Harlem congressman—threatened King, in a complicated power play, with revealing that he and Rustin were lovers. This was entirely absurd (King's tastes did not that way run), but it scared the daylights out of King because the accusation of homosexuality was so toxic at that time—and the double whammy of commie and queer, directed at Rustin, was seen as disqualifying. (LBJ's top aide, Walter Jenkins, was ruined by being found in a YMCA with another man.) Stanley Levison, the ex-Communist whom Rustin had introduced to King, sneered and later said that Rustin was "better qualified to lead a homosexual movement than a civil rights movement"—this sounds prescient now but was wholly pejorative then. It led King to cruelly drive Rustin away. Rustin was broken and devastated by the split. But a couple of years later, as the idea for a great march on Washington began to brew, Rustin was the only one thought competent to lead it. At first reluctantly, through Randolph's insistence, and then more and more gratefully, Rustin arrived to organize it.

When people say that Rustin was the mastermind behind the 1963 March on Washington (Dr. King basically arrived to give a speech in the place that Rustin had assigned for him), what they mean can seem nebulous. He *thought* of it? No, what he did was to *organize* it. He worked day and night with a team of kids on West 130th Street to make it happen. It was exhaustingly particular. Dr. King, as Rustin once memorably said, "did not have the ability to organize vampires to go to a bloodbath." Because American progressivism is, alongside French conservatism, the most schismatic of all faiths, with lifelong resentments governing everyone in turn and new schisms springing up every minute, Rustin had to exert a full court press to bring everyone together. "We planned out precisely the number of toilets that would be needed for a quarter of a million people, how many blankets . . . how many doctors, how many first aid stations, what people would bring with them to eat in their lunches. Plan it so that everybody would come in to Washington after dark the night before, and everybody would be out of Washington by sundown on the day of the march."

After the march his homosexuality, his refusal to narrow the civil rights struggle down to an ethnic or racial cause, and his wisdom that what he called confrontational politics was the opiate of the self-deluded left—he thought that the slogan black power was limiting and self-destructive—left him marginalized but marginalized in a positive way, as a kind of minister without portfolio for the left. He committed to the Democratic Party, very much as Frederick Douglass had remained committed to the left-wing of the old Republican Party, creating impatience among the next generation who thought he was too old to "get it" any longer.

Though an apostle of egalitarian social reform, he also eventually became avid for the last clause in our liberal-rhino sentence: the need for an ever-greater tolerance of human differences. Early on, he seems to have felt that asserting his gay identity too openly would stand in the way of the common cause of civil rights. In his later years, he accepted his sexuality as an important truth about himself. He knew that the tension between the move toward equality and the move toward self-expression is not a contradiction in liberalism. It's the claim liberalism makes: that we can express ourselves while expanding the right to access a broader range of pleasures and possibilities for other people. Liberals want both and don't see these goals as a contradiction but as the same task—just as a tightrope walker experiences no "contradiction" between staying on the tightrope and walking forward on it. Staying on the wire

77

despite the difficulty of keeping your balance is the whole reason you became a tightrope walker. It's the point of the act. The point of the liberal act is to expand freedom while also expanding equality. You lean a little to the left and a little to the right and sometimes a flock of monkeys drops on your shoulders—as happens to Charlie Chaplin in *The Circus*—and you have to keep walking anyway. Keeping your balance is the point, not the problem. (It is perhaps not entirely an accident that one of Lincoln's favorite metaphors for the liberal politicians' task was to compare it to that of the tightrope walker Charles Blondin, making his way across Niagara Falls.)

Rustin, like Montaigne or Mill or Eliot, was many things at once. He spoke of himself by turns as a liberal, a radical, a socialist, and a world citizen. But his commitment to liberal institutions and practices was absolute. It was one of the reasons why—and some of his present biographers seem puzzled by the force of his repudiation of left totalitarianism, as though he were merely a cold warrior—he was, despite being persecuted as a red by Hoover and the FBI, resolutely anti-Communist. He recognized that without liberal institutions there was no possibility of democratic reform. As late as 1986, he could write, "I do not believe that freedom and economic justice are incompatible. This is not to say that we have fully achieved freedom and economic justice in the United States. We have not. But here we have the freedom to argue and fight for justice in the press, in the courts and on the streets . . . I know from personal experience that civil rights workers here were jailed and some were killed. I have been arrested 24 times working for civil rights in this country. I am aware of the undemocratic excesses of individual policemen, Mr. Nixon and the FBI . . . the difference between being a dissident, civil rights worker or social reformer here and the Soviet Union has to do with the penalties for such activity. Every time I was arrested and imprisoned here, there were committees organized on my behalf to defend me . . . [wrongdoing by the government is] documented in the press, investigated by governmental and non-governmental agencies and challenged in the courts." Humane ideals could only be made into working rules through liberal institutions.

You may ask, though, as others have: wasn't Rustin "really" a leftist radical who forced reluctant liberals to act? The answer—and on this even a liberal can be unequivocal—is no. His was an activism always imagined on specifically liberal terms, liberal activism at its most potent. It's why he insisted that organized nonviolent demonstrations were the opposite of riots, not their threatening prelude. It's why, at considerable cost to his reputation and influence, he rejected again and again the narrow constraints of a merely racial militancy. It's why he believed in the American Constitution, no matter how often it disappointed his causes.

Rustin was a liberal activist in his firm commitment to liberal institutions but also in his possession of an almost perfect liberal temperament. He wanted to seed the world with sanity. What makes his letters to his brutal jailors so moving is that he appeals to them as ordinary men with ordinary desires.

There is no more hard-won endorsement of the dispersal of power and authority that are central to liberalism than his. Making individuals free while making the institutions protecting freedom stronger was for Rustin a double and inseparable cause. If anyone deserves the title of radical of the real, it is him.

∾◌◠

What is liberalism, then? A hatred of cruelty. An instinct about human conduct rooted in a rueful admission of our own fallibility and of the inadequacy of our divided minds to be right frequently enough to act autocratically. A belief that the sympathy that binds human society together can disconnect us from our clannish and suspicious past. A program for permanent reform based on reason and an appeal to argument, aware of human fallibility and open to the lessons of experience. An understanding that small, open social institutions, if no larger than a café or more overtly political than a park, play an outsized role in creating free minds and securing public safety. A faith in rational debate, rather than inherited ritual, and in reform, rather than either revolution or reaction. A belief in radical change through practial measures. A readiness to act—nonviolently but visibly and sometimes in the face of threatened violence—on behalf of equality. A belief that life should be fair—or fairer, or as fair as seems fair: people's lives should not be overdetermined by who their parents were or how much money they might have inherited or what shade of skin their genes have woven. A belief that the individual pursuit of eccentric happiness can be married to a common faith in fair procedure.

All this imagined, yes, with a strong though not decisive materialist bent—based on faith in worldly pleasure, a belief that whatever spiritual rewards or pursuits might give our finite lives greater meaning, none of them mean much if people are not fed and housed and taught and, to some degree or another, tickled. (With this, though, a recognition that great movements of reform have, as often as not, begun in churches as much as clubs.)

These values are rooted in a simple moral idea about human capacity—a moral idea about the source of meaning in the individual imagination. This just means that people make up their values, that they aren't handed down from the past or from on high. This humanist ideal is what intersects and animates liberalism with moral energy. The opposite of humanism is not theism but fanaticism; the opposite of liberalism is not conservatism but dogmatism. Fanaticism is therefore the chief enemy of humanism, and fanaticism in political life is the chief enemy of the liberal ideal.

Liberalism believes in the imperfectability of mankind. It is a perpetual program of reform intended to alleviate the cruelty we see around us. The result will not be a perfect society but merely another society, with its own unanticipated defects to correct, though with some of the worst injustices—tearing limbs from people or keeping them as chattel or depriving half the population of the right to speak to their own future—gone, we hope for good. That is as close as liberalism gets to a utopian vision: a future society that is flawed, like our own, but less cruel as time goes on.

Smith and Hume, Lewes and Eliot, Mill and Taylor, Rustin and Montaigne, Olmsted and Putnam share a belief in social conversation as an antidote to authority and a belief that reforming the world takes work but is worth it. They made philosophies, built parks, wrote novels, edited journals, led demonstrations, designed and carried out empirical studies, and sometimes did truly great things that did not always look great to their contemporaries. Their accomplishments often had little to do with conventional ideas of success. One was a bad mayor in a corrupt regime, another an unsuccessful member of Parliament, one other a depressed playground designer. None of them had an all-purpose explanation of everything. Each focused on a place or a part of the whole.

And yet the constellation of ideas and values and processes and principles that they embodied and helped make, despite creating more plural and peaceful and prosperous societies than any other social practice known to history, is under constant assault today, from intellectuals and ordinary people alike. Why? What are the strong arguments against liberal democratic politics as we recognize it and against the liberal humanist values that underlie it? Where can they be found, what do they argue, and how can they be answered?

CHAPTER TWO

WHY THE RIGHT HATES LIBERALISM

THERE ARE the ideas of liberalism, defined anew: an ongoing and evolving campaign for mostly egalitarian reform achieved through open discussion and debate, often rising from small dissenting communities to create pluralist institutions—liberal institutions. We've seen how liberalism is not centrism in any sense but rather a form of radical realism responsible for almost all the humane changes that the Western world has seen in the past two hundred years. The liberation of women, the emancipation of slaves and then of the racially oppressed, the recognition of the rights of sexual minorities—these are all the unique achievements of liberal states, engineered by liberal activists, all things that have never happened before in history.

With that record—and on the whole a record of peace and prosperity, again unique in history—why, then, is liberalism so set upon, so broadly unpopular in so many ways? Two ferocious critiques, one from the left and one from the right, exist to explain it. And, yes, being a liberal means being perpetually engaged in a two-front war, like Hercules with the two snakes in his birth cradle, one in his right hand, the other in his left.

What are the two serpents? I said before that liberalism is rooted in a belief in reform and reason. The right-wing critique of liberalism is largely an attack on its overreliance on *reason*; the left-wing one, mostly an attack on its false faith in *reform*. The right-wing assault also tends to focus on the evil that liberalism does *internally* to the traditional communities and nations it betrays; the left wing pays attention, as well, and sometimes more often, to the evil that liberalism does *externally* to its distant victims in the foreign countries it exploits. Liberalism, on both views, is the Cuisinart of culture, whipping around and pureeing what had once been coherent communities. The left says it does this mostly in pursuit of profit and on behalf of the capitalism that liberalism shelters (even as it smiles and pretends it does not); the right, that it does this in pursuit of perverse principles and on behalf of the monster state that liberalism idealizes (even as it frowns and pretends to love only freedom).

Nothing's more central to the liberal ideal than a belief in debate, a belief that airing differences actually gets you somewhere new. Mill himself said that social life is made up of conflicting half-truths, not absolutes anyone owns. So, let's take each case against liberalism in turn and try to present it as seriously and sympathetically as we can. And let's be clear at once that a philosophy of right-wing politics and even of reactionary authoritarianism exists that is not merely paid hate literature. This seems like a minimal admission, but it is an essential one. Many liberals and lefties assume that conservative ideas are not much more than a series of sham apologias in which well-paid scribes write whatever their wealthy bosses at Fox News or at Koch Industries want them to write. What's called conservative philosophy is, according to this view, really only advertising for the entrenched order. The model of this kind is the career of Ronald Reagan at General Electric in the 1950s. Reagan, a New Deal liberal in his earlier life, was hired by General Electric to go out and shill for corporate capitalism. He did, and a political star was born. Had the AFL-CIO had enough money to pay him, the logic goes, we might in 1980 have elected a social democrat—or else we would have elected some other movie actor, next on GE's list. This may be unfair to Ronald Reagan, who was heading right anyway and had views and instincts of his own, but more important I think it's unfair to conservatism. There is no shortage of cogent arguments against liberalism from the right as much as from the left.

Indeed, the primary argument is simple and compelling: the most important need human beings have is for *order*. Order not merely in their daily lives but in their world. Without order, everything collapses. The order may come down from God and be "natural," or it may be artificial and made up, but it is essential. Liberalism, with its emphasis on reform, is an instrument of rapid change, the conservative says. And change disorders order. Change *risks* order, and then only later realizes what the loss of order has cost ordinary people. Order does not just mean obedience to authority, though at times it does mean accepting a subordinate role for ourselves for the good of everyone else. Order means disciplining our desires—in ways that liberals may not always like—to assure that social peace can continue. It may mean sometimes keeping quiet about our deepest beliefs, rather than risk starting a civil war. It might require avoiding conflict at all costs even when we think we're right.

The conservative's concern over order implies knowledge about what actually happens when social order breaks down. The value of order is perhaps more evident to those who have not had order in their lives than it is to those who have lived with a superfluity of it. You do not have to explain to Tutsis in Rwanda the value of the police. And lest one think that this is merely the bullying creed of tyrants, large and small, both the Caesars and Gottis of the world—or too closely allied to the American right-wing code of law and order—we should recall that the most widely human of all poets thinks this, too. Again and again, Shakespeare, who had come of age in a time of violent civil and religious war, extolls the necessity of order; he hates tyranny, but what worries him is anarchy and strife. Shakespeare, for whom nothing human ever is alien, embraced Montaigne's insight that human beings are cracked in two by nature, but he also understood the need for order to keep all those cracked eggs from running all over each other. Two of the greatest set piece orations in all of Shakespeare—the Archbishop of Canterbury's speech about the lesson of the beehive in *Henry V* and Ulysses's speech on order in *Troilus and Cressida*—take as their subjects the beauty and necessity of order and of degree, meaning inherited hierarchy. When Shakespeare sings, he sings most eloquently about the beauty of an ordered and hierarchical world not for the sake of the powerful but for those beneath them. For without degree, Ulysses tells us:

> Force should be right; or rather, right and wrong,
> Between whose endless jar justice resides,
> Should lose their names, and so should justice too.

Then everything includes itself in power,
Power into will, will into appetite;
And appetite, a universal wolf,
So doubly seconded with will and power,
Must make perforce a universal prey,
And last eat up himself.

"Power into will, will into appetite; And appetite a universal wolf," devouring all. This is as good a capsule description of the history of Nazism or Stalinism as one can imagine: first the thirst for power, then the pure assertion of will, and then the world wolfed down, large and small alike. Shakespeare believed in charity and forgiveness, too—justice and order tempered by mercy and cheer. But the risk of the universal wolf unleashed when every station in life is contested worried him far more. Shakespeare himself was a simple boy from the middle classes, courting the wealthy in London—but the passion and eloquence of his hymns makes it plain that he was not writing to command but from conviction. Untune the lute of life, and discord follows.

Nor, to leap ahead in time, could Edmund Burke or Samuel Johnson, both eighteenth-century London authors and passionate conservative voices, derive for themselves any special advantage from sponsoring a society of fixed degree, born as they were well outside it. Their convictions were as real as Shakespeare's and cemented in the same knowledge—theirs more bookish, perhaps, than the Bard's—of what happens in a city when there is no policeman on the beat. (There *were* no policemen on the beat in their time, and the young impoverished Dr. Johnson ended up having to clobber a few would-be muggers by himself.) A love of order can be felt just as strongly by the impoverished as the insolent; in fact, Johnson thought, the impoverished need order *more*, since they have fewer means for buying themselves out of natural anarchy.

Conservative philosophy, in other words, is, as we say now, a thing and deserves a serious listen. Yet conservatism is in many ways an even more confusing term than *liberalism*, taking in everyone from upright patricians to down-home fundamentalist preachers. Even conservative superstars can be confounding. Burke, as hallowed a name among the right as Mill is among liberals, actually spent most of his parliamentary life arguing in favor of the great liberal revolution of his day, the American one, and trying to impeach Warren Hastings, the brutal colonial ruler of India, on behalf of the imperialized and oppressed—as though a contemporary conservative politician would devote his career to pursuing the Blackwater mercenaries in Iraq for war crimes.

Among right-wing critics of liberalism, the emphasis on social order is grounded in something still more primal: a reverence for the natural order of family and community. So, let's begin to clarify the right-wing critique with another image. Remember, Olivia, when you and I went out for dinner at that nice Persian restaurant on Second Avenue after you had done some competitive exam—SATs or ACTs or another—and how there was this huge family at the next table? And how we envied the intensity of their engagement with each other, moms and dads and patriarchs and matriarchs, all eating and arguing together? They shared plates, ignored children, yelled and hugged and raised hell. We seemed so . . . atomized, so alone, by comparison.

We said at the time that it was striking—and disturbing— that though I come from a very big family where there are no particularly grievous feuds among its members, we only get together once every ten years or so. We enjoy each other. But great periods of time will go by when my five siblings and thirty-some nieces and nephews never glimpse one another—because we're all off pursuing our meritocratic careers at one end or another of the continent, or even in Australia, while our poor plaintive parents wait home in Canada for us to call. A strong clan identity—though visible in some subtle ways—is not something we can retreat into very easily for comfort. Our comforts lie in achievement, rather than in communality.

And as you said to me shrewdly at the time, in the absence of clan feeling, the nuclear family—we four—become ever more important as a kind of life raft in the ocean of existence. Perhaps *too* important. Upper-middle-class people overinvest in one or two kids rather than broadly investing in many generations, as most human beings throughout time have done, and this overinvestment, a frequent argument goes, is hugely destructive to society at large, since it makes them ferociously desperate to reserve the same places for their kids that they have been occupying, leaving no room for others to join in or up. (I used to joke mordantly that the two of us ran a little money-losing boutique business, with two employees with great health and educational benefits.)

All conservative critiques of liberalism, both the essentially respectful loyal opposition kind and the violent and enraged kind that marks modern authoritarian movements, begin here. They say that liberalism is the natural enemy of community, and of the families and traditions that make communities stable, and that stable communities are essential to happy lives. The liberty and freedom liberalism emphasizes leave its adherents with an atomized existence, fragmented and unfulfilling and, in a certain sense, inhumane. Even the nuclear family is a kind of steel cocoon around our essential loneliness, hard shells around organized ambition. The way we live in modern countries, stripped of the traditional order of common fates, identity, and meaning, is not how people ought to live. Politics in one way or other needs to restore that order.

This is a predicament far better caught and crystallized in art than argued in polemics. It is a truth about our country that can take a poignant turn. In Barry Levinson's beautiful too-little-seen movie *Avalon*, Sam, the immigrant patriarch, arrives as a young man in a still-thriving Baltimore, where he makes a rich and complex family and clan life until, step by step, modernity strips away the generations and meaning from his life, and he is left utterly alone, watching television in a single room in an assisted-living home. That's the Pyrrhic triumph of liberalism: we invite people in to make their lives, and then abandon them as they become unproductive. We break apart the family and call it self-fulfillment; take away the common table, and call it progress.

~❦~

Order, in both the family and in society, is the concern uniting conservatives, and liberal reform its natural enemy. But, again, there are many varieties of conservatives, perhaps more than of liberals, and their attacks on liberalism are almost as varied.

Before we look at the really radical attacks, we should look at the more neighborly critique of liberalism from what we might call the constitutional conservatives. By constitutional conservatives, I mean the old responsible-government core of the Republican Party (yes, it once existed) or the Conservative parties in Britain and Canada or the various Christian Democratic parties in Europe; they have been in power more often than not in the liberal era. What do they believe that's different enough from liberals to make them want to passionately distinguish themselves, even if they, too, agree on the centrality of individual rights and democracy?

Most often, they will say that they believe in strong armies, low taxes, and, perhaps above all, limited government. Permit me to be skeptical about this self-description. I don't actually think that limited or large government matters as much in distinguishing contemporary liberals from constitutional conservatives as we are told it does. All of us want just as large a government as suits the current needs of our values and programs. Statism may or may not be a sin, but if it is, it is a sin neither of liberal left nor liberalish right. Liberals want government to be large enough, for instance, to enforce gun control laws, but not intrusive enough to have anything to do with women and their reproductive choices.

Conservatives in power may want to reduce government in some of its roles—in how we regulate businesses or workplace safety or the environment—but they invariably increase the power of government in some other roles: taxing for the military, or policing immigration, or, perhaps, surreptitiously subsidizing favored energy industries. Nothing could be more of a big government program than the capital punishment that delights so many American conservatives. Indeed, there is nothing that is such an obscene parody of the liberal administrative state as the American way of killing convicts—the poison to be introduced into the veins after they have been strapped down helpless to a gurney must not have passed its due by date for fear of an accident. We have to be sure that every paper is stamped correctly and only then can we kill. Certainly, if the pro-life movement has any serious purpose—and I think it does—it would require a pregnancy police force, tracking women and prosecuting doctors for clandestine abortions. That was the policing practice not so very long ago, and it drove abortion, which will always be a fact of human life, underground. So I don't believe that distinction really holds.

What *actually* and effectively separates liberal and mainstream conservative parties and politicians, seen squarely, are certain ideas about respect and certain rituals of reverence—particularly respect for the military and reverence for religion. This is the outward show of order. Indeed, we can go back to a crucial moment in mid-nineteenth-century Britain when those two things—liberalism for the first time called as such and conservatism evolving into a now-familiar direction—took on their distinctive characters and see how much the differences between them already depended on these rituals of reverence.

That story is tied to the lives of two of the greatest characters in the history of democracy: Benjamin Disraeli and William Ewart Gladstone. They were the premier political figures of their time: Disraeli as the leader of the Conservative Party in the House of Commons and Gladstone as one of the first leaders of the Liberal Party, properly so called. They are an endlessly fascinating pair, whose lives tell us much about the temperament essential for liberals and conservatives—temperament being at least as important as fixed principles for analyzing the kinds—and how those temperaments do and don't become principles.

The joke is that while Gladstone, the liberal, was a conservative-minded man of pious intentions and impeccable Christian faith—though with a piety speckled by an undue curiosity in "rescuing" fallen women while roaming the streets of London—he became liberal by virtue of his distaste of privilege. He mistrusted the inherited rights of the landed gentry, whom he respected as individuals but disliked as a group. Though he was himself paternalistic in manner—he would be a university dean today—he genuinely wanted to end privileged institutions. (So much so that he inspired Lewis Carroll, who was Toryish in politics, to two anagrams on his name, in weird despair at Gladstone's radicalism: "Wilt tear down all images?" And, even better, "Wild agitator! Means well.")

Disraeli, the great Conservative leader, was just the opposite. He was gay, overdressed, and Jewish. (Though he wasn't out as a homosexual in our sense, of course, few could, or did, miss his devotion to a string of handsome younger men nor his companionate marriage to a rich older woman.) His Jewishness, meanwhile, though theatrically obliterated by baptism, was the most obvious thing about him, so much so that Otto von Bismarck, the Prussian strongman, called him simply "the old Jew." He was also a satiric novelist and mischievous to a point of perversity. Imagine, a gay Jewish Tom Wolfe becoming the Republican candidate for president. He wore wild brocaded vests and golden pocket watches and all the rest of the regalia of a dandy. Yet, he came to lead the party of the landed gentry, who mistrusted him, and helped fashion the rhetoric of what we think of as modern, mainstream conservatism.

Disraeli saw that the right-wing land-owning classes in England had a message that might speak to people outside their immediate circle of fellow landowners. "Young England" was the smart name he chose for his new movement; even though the youth in question were all landed gentry, it sounded dashing. Against the Manchester School of industrial capitalists who were perceived as undermining traditional society, Disraeli's new ideology—which he pretty much foisted onto a set of surprised Bertie Woosters who were too hungover to know they had one—was a kind of neomedievalism, full of imaginary images of a lost Camelot of England. But neomedievalism as a repository of ideas, or, really, a pageant of emotions, was a hugely rich vein of feeling. It appealed to left and right and center—to everyone who felt that modern, Manchesterized life was erasing the beautiful details of British tradition.

Disraeli understood that an appeal to national grandeur would be wildly popular, and not just among those whose interests it protected and whom he in a sense represented—the aristocrats who used him rather as one might hire a clever lawyer. (Although they soon found that the clever lawyer was using them.) He was among the first to spot a vulnerability that we can call a vulnerability of identity. He understood that a traditional appeal to a reverence for the nation—which in England's case, at the time, meant reverence for the empire, which is to say the nation's "achievements"—was essential to a broadly based democracy. In his years in office in the 1870s he built up an elaborate cult of Queen Victoria—not especially popular earlier in her reign—as the empress of India and the embodiment of the imperial mission. He arranged for England to buy a stake in the Suez Canal, and did as much as he could to design and enforce a regal symbolism that extended beyond the monarch. Gladstone, in turn, was a liberal internationalist *avant la lettre*, in favor of an intervention on humanitarian grounds in the "Bulgarian horrors" committed by the Ottomans in the 1870s. But he was not a natural regalist.

It was Disraeli's guess that an enfranchised working population would be as likely to support imperialist pride as social solidarity, and it turned out to be one of the shrewdest guesses in the history of modern political life. It confounded the expectations of his contemporaries, and it continues to confound liberals and the left to this day. Why aren't the people sharing our values if they share our problems? The white working class is working class in the first instance; they must *really* want to side with social democrats if only they could be shown the way.

It never happens. It doesn't because identity, or national pride if you prefer, has proven time and again to be incomparably more powerful than economic self-interest narrowly defined. Why jingoism should be of such overwhelming appeal to the working classes, easily trumping apparently obvious differences in interests between themselves and the economic imperialists, is a central mystery of the modern age, at least to liberals. One would think that conquering Burma would be of as little significance to a cockney as winning Afghanistan would be now to his descendant, but it is so: popular imperialism is the cosmopolitanism of the poor, the lever by which the small and impotent come to believe that their acts have world historical meaning. The true interests of the people are defined by the people, and class interests tend to be secondary to national pride.

This is a lesson liberals and the left perpetually forget and have to be perpetually retaught. As Disraeli put it himself, with prescient clarity, "In a progressive country change is constant; and the great question is, not whether you should resist change which is inevitable, but whether that change should be carried out in deference to the manners, the customs, the laws, the traditions of the people, or in deference to abstract principles and arbitrary and general doctrines."

You recall the London sewer system that G. H. Lewes and his generation fought so hard to obtain? Well, though it was in origin a liberal program, argued for on pragmatic reformist grounds, it was Disraeli who was in power when, in 1858, London finally began a massive public sewer system to protect it from its own waste—and from the miasma, and cholera, the waste produced. Regal means and rational measures: it is not a bad definition of the best side of the conservative imagination in the modern world.

So, Gladstone, a man of instinctive liberal and egalitarian temperament, ended up doing a lot of important conservative work, setting the exemplar for the kind of pugnacious nation building and moral interventionism that neoconservatives in America not so long ago still loved. Disraeli, a man of instinctive conservative and romantic temperament, ended up doing a lot of the work of liberalism—knowing that it would work for his cause, he bulled through mass enfranchisement, in addition to endorsing and even engineering essential public works programs—so much that he could, almost, register as a liberal hero, if the idea would not so badly shock his ghost.

The idea of showing deference to the manners and traditions of a people—or part of a people anyway—is essential to the project of modern conservatism and makes it part of the strength of the modern liberal state. Disraeli began a potent tradition in which a politics of national grandeur was not opposed to the practices of liberal democracy and could fit within it and often triumph.

To take another heroic insistence of the same traditionalist but firmly democratic kind, we might look to Winston Churchill or, better yet, turn to the figure of Charles de Gaulle, whose fidelity to liberal institutions was bought at a much higher cost in a much more resistant environment than Churchill's.

For de Gaulle is, perhaps above all, a significant figure for the sincerity and endurance of his republicanism: from a background that in most places and circumstances would have led, in crisis, toward some form of Bonapartism, he became and remained a faithful believer in free elections and in submitting to the will of the people. He held dear "a certain idea of France," to use his famous phrase, but it was a *republican* idea of France. His story embodies the idea of a principled, conservative, and regal-style politics, completely distinct in tone from liberalism but in many ways just as committed to democracy.

Although he insisted that his origins were among the country gentry, in fact he was raised in Paris's Seventh Arrondissement, which combines both the aristocratic Faubourg St. Germain and the great military institutions—the École Militaire and the Invalides soldiers' hospital. It was then a place, as he put it perfectly, marked by a "military melancholy," of a spacious sadness of grand and empty green spaces. De Gaulle's reactionary politics, learned from his parents, were humanized by a dense literary culture. "The most wonderful job in the world would be as a librarian," de Gaulle said once. He was being puckish but not entirely so. He knew Corneille by heart and could quote his plays. He had absorbed the lesson of tragedy: that most hopes are doomed, that all choices come at a cost, that enduring loss with dignity is the highest of human callings. When the worst happened and the German tank corps overran France in the spring of 1940, de Gaulle felt not only that his talents had been misused but, worse for a Frenchman of intellect, that his theories had been ignored. "Our initial defeat," he wrote in a memorandum whose effect on his desperate superiors one can only wonder at, "comes from the application by the enemy of ideas that are mine."

He escaped the Germans in 1940 with little more than a paltry title and the clothes on his back. In exile in London, de Gaulle strikingly changed his views from those of a normal French officer, with understandable contempt for the squabbling, mediocre politicians of the Third Republic, to a kind of determined republicanism. He came to understand that only revolutionary republican values could speak to and for France.

De Gaulle came to see that the republic and its magic words *liberty, equality,* and *fraternity*—not the near-Vichyite ones of *fatherland* and *family,* which he had first favored— would alone serve France in all its fullness. He was the farthest thing in the world from an instinctive democrat, but he didn't have to be. It was enough that he understood that democracy had become one of the instincts of France.

He returned to power after the war, during the Algerian crisis of 1958, to found the Fifth Republic. Its secret, as with Disraeli's Victorian rule, was that beneath the sonorous grandiosity and medievalist rhetoric, the new regime was entirely technocratic and reformist. He put France on the path to modernization as Disraeli had done a century before for Britain.

The central political idea that de Gaulle intuited was the one he shared with Disraeli: myths matter. Without a sense of common significance and shared symbols, it is impossible for any modern state to go on. National dignity is absolutely central to any program of national renewal. (Had American policy toward Russia post-1989 been shaped with an eye not just to that country's political system but to its pride—to making sure that the Russians had a myth of their own self-liberation, instead of being so obviously plundered and defeated—the ensuing disaster could, conceivably, have been less disastrous.) De Gaulle crafted a symbolic history for the French in place of a real one because the symbols were among the most real things they knew.

The distinction that's sometimes made between patriotism and nationalism is the essence of de Gaulle's politics, as it had been in many ways of Disraeli's. The patriot loves his place and its monarch and its cheeses and its people and its idiosyncrasies; the nationalist has no particular sense of affection for the actual place he advocates for (he is often an outsider to it) but employs his obsessive sense of encirclement and grievance on behalf of acts of ethnic vengeance. With his love of honor and pageantry, de Gaulle might seem to offer a very dated model of politics. And yet in an odd way, there's an urgent, living lesson for the twenty-first century in what de Gaulle accomplished that can't be overlooked. The politics of national grandeur, he showed, need not be the exclusive province of bullies and gangsters and crooks and clowns. It's a fine French lesson.

Liberals on the whole are more skeptical of such emotions and images, or at least more embarrassed in their presence, even when, as often happens, they actually inhabit those traditions just as fully—as on, for instance, the Fourth of July in the United States. No political battle could be more telling on this point than the moment Ronald Reagan unseated Jimmy Carter in the presidential election of 1980. Carter had, in fact, begun a program of deregulation of such things as the airline industry that would later become emblematic of the free-market turn of Reaganism. Carter was both a career naval officer and a man of deep abiding faith. But he and his party had a hard time dramatizing these emotions, while Reagan, who had never spent a day in uniform and was cheerfully indifferent to church, knew instinctively how to dramatize those emotions, how to look snappy saluting, and how to invoke the Almighty as needed, with results we know.

The conservative's emphasis on social order and national myths leads him, even if he is a constitutional conservative like Disraeli or de Gaulle who accepts liberal institutions (indeed, they think that they understand liberal institutions better than the liberals who have perverted them), to object to the liberal's perpetual use of government for reform. For the conservative, reforms produce the need for more reforms not because, as the liberal says, new problems emerge but because the reform has *created* problems, which would never have happened if we had just left well enough alone.

We can now come back to Edmund Burke and our first confusion about the meaning of conservatism—for Burke, for all his liberalism, became what we now call a conservative exactly on these questions: a reverence for the regal and a concern that big bad enlightened ideas, and the supposed reforms that flowed from them, were perverting the natural order. Burke, as we've said, spent half his political life endorsing the revolution in America and then another huge chunk of it prosecuting Warren Hastings, the British boss in India accused of cruelty to the "natives." These were very much what we would now call liberal causes, directed on humane principles against oligarchic power. But when the French Revolution happened, Burke recoiled in horror, not principally at the mass killings during the reign of terror, which actually only really began after he wrote, but at the regicide of Louis XVI. Burke's most famous words, tellingly, were for the king's wife, writing of the (at best) pathetic Marie Antoinette that "I thought ten thousand swords must have leaped from their scabbards, to avenge even a look that threatened her with insult. But the age of chivalry is gone. That of sophisters, economists, and calculators has succeeded; and the glory of Europe is extinguished forever. Never, never more, shall we behold that generous loyalty to rank and sex, that proud submission, that dignified obedience, that subordination of the heart, which kept alive, even in servitude itself, the spirit of an exalted freedom."

The idea that the appearance of submission and obedience and rank are essential to order is at the heart of the conservative ideal—even when practical politics may lead elsewhere. Burke wasn't just offended by the violence done to many; he was terrified of the violence done to kings and queens, since it decapitated the very idea of social order. The people who cut the king's head off were in the grip of a big idea so intoxicating that it annihilated their ability to see past their own bloodlust. The abstract principle of enlightenment egalitarianism, led by rational intellectuals, "economists and calculators," indifferent to the actual fate of individuals, had combined with a belief in the necessity of radical reform to destroy a revered tradition. Burke becomes a modern conservative in this moment. Tom Paine was horrified at the killing of the king and queen because he knew how the murder would diminish the dignity of the French Revolution; Burke was horrified because of how it would diminish the dignity of kings.

❧

The quarrel between constitutional conservatives and liberals can be bitter and profound—the difference between

Carter and Reagan was enormous, and the perpetual argument between Burke and Mill is real—but it takes place within a general agreement that the rules of parliamentary democracy, even in the nascent state that Burke knew them, are essentially a sound way of sorting out their quarrels, with at least a minimal agreement that an oscillation of power between the two sides is inevitable.

But Burke's horrified reaction to the killing of the French king and queen helps point us toward another, far fiercer right-wing critique of liberalism. That assault finds in liberalism a fatal overreliance on reason. It shares Burke's sense of the chaos that could follow from the belief that society should be remade all at once on the basis of a big idea, with tradition and custom annihilated. Such conservatives recall the clan at its common table and note its absence in the liberal imagination and think this far worse than a mere periodically adjustable change of emphasis. They see in liberalism a moral atrocity and a practical failure, a baleful compendium of bad ideas.

We can list them. There is liberal *secularism*, the indifference to faith that calls itself "toleration" but is really intolerance for anything that lies beyond liberal understanding, treating millennial-old beliefs as though they were as disposable as Kleenex, and with those unsure about the sudden new secular wisdom treated not as skeptics but as haters and bigots. There is liberal *cosmopolitanism*, the indifference to national loyalty that makes liberals easily contemplate going elsewhere and, worse still, welcoming in the world through unsifted immigration. There is liberal *permissiveness*, the disdain for simple moral ideas—as simple, say, as the one that says that all children should have a father and a mother to bring them up—that thrills those cosmopolitans but brings misery and despair to working people. And, lest we forget, there is liberal *relativism*, the insistence that you have your way and I have my own, and if yours involves having sex with cocker spaniels, have at it, what business is it of mine? Secularism, cosmopolitanism, permissiveness, relativism: these are things that liberals boast of as positive values, while their catastrophic effects on ordinary people and their lives is self-evident. Communities gasp and die while cosmopolitans just move elsewhere for their next party.

Some version or another of this kind of communitarian complaint is at the heart of the more benign interpretations of the crisis of what's called populism, the rise of Trump, and the success of Brexit. Whole communities, entire cities, are being stripped of their identity and history—by the relentless march of capitalism, yes, but also by a cultural elite in London or New York or Paris or Palo Alto that looks down its nose at anyone left behind and tries to impose its ideas on them. Reduced to despair by the loss of all familiar certainties, a majority of ordinary people lash out at an establishment that shows so little empathy with their existence, even if it means choosing an irrational-seeming course like isolation from Europe or embracing an obvious gangster-clown like Trump. The obviousness of the clownishness, the supposed irrationality of the Brexit choice, are exactly what makes them attractive—lets rub the elite's noses in the awfulness they dread, and they who have ignored our truths might at last share a little in our misery. Liberal-minded people are understandably suspicious of this interpretation: they think that economic anxiety is a nice name for hard-core and persistent bigotry. But the choice between economic anxiety and outright bigotry is very likely a false one: people often articulate economic anxiety *as* bigotry and, as often, explain their instinctive bigotry to themselves as economic anxiety.

Here again, writers and artists may have more to tell us than polemicists. Certainly, of all the accounts of this process I've read, the best—better even than *Hillbilly Elegy*, the memoir by J. D. Vance—is by Chrissie Hynde, the pop singer who founded The Pretenders, in her autobiography *Reckless*. It's an interestingly unreckless book. Growing up in Akron, Ohio, in the fifties and sixties (yeah, I, too, thought she was British), she got to participate in a genuinely rich and diverse urban culture. There were lunch counters, soda fountains, and department stores to enjoy and, as she got older, indie record stores and jazz clubs to relish as well. There were places for teenagers to run to and others for grown-ups to rub elbows in. There was a busy train station and regular train service.

All of this, within a startlingly short time, between the seventies and nineties, was rubbed right out of existence by the decline of the Akron tire manufacturing business and the abandonment of its dependent industries. Within fifteen years, Akron had rusted away. Hynde writes: "A suffocating cloak of isolation was enveloping America. Only the 'destination places,' cultural centers you visit or pass through . . . still functioned, and defined the seclusion that was spreading like molten lava. Akron was now just one of tens of thousands of cities being subsumed into metroplexes, a sinister alchemy at play. The creed was 'every man for himself.'" The jazz clubs were gone, all the hotels had closed, and the trains stopped running. And everyone was left alone or feeling so.

Every man for himself. It is easy to say that these devastating transformations are part of the natural process of change in a free-market society—but this does not alter the recurrent crisis of this kind of loss, which could be duplicated instantly in far-off seeming cities like Lille in the north of France, a hotbed of the National Front, or by once thriving towns like Blackpool and Salford in the north of England, places that voted overwhelmingly for Brexit. It is easy for metropolitans to shrug and say it was not of our liberal doing, but if we want to take pride in what liberalism has accomplished, we have to take responsibility for what it *does*. Free societies crush community? Hmmm. Should we not, perhaps, then query the meaning of free?

⁂

What makes the radical right-wing communitarian complaint distinct from the left-wing attack on liberalism—which blames capitalism for all this human pain, first and last—is that it almost always places the blame for the loss of identity on the loss of *authority*. And it blames liberal *ideas* (from secularism to relativism) more than it tends to blame free-market economics—which the right, for the most part with some significant exceptions, usually embraces, too—for the disasters of modern life. The right, partly for reasons of convenience—they tend to be funded by the corporate people who helped ruin Akron—but largely for reasons of conviction, believe that it is liberal elites, not capitalism, that are most to blame for the destruction of community.

Globalization may have despoiled Akron; it was liberal elites who demoralized its people. Walmart may have helped ruin Main Street, but it was the liberal monopoly in education and entertainment that destroyed the social capital that Main Streeters had painfully accumulated over generations. They were manipulated by the plutocrats of Walmart, and then mocked by the graduates of Wesleyan. (The National Front in France says that the same thing is true for the people of Lille considering the elites in Paris; they were first abandoned to open immigration and then ridiculed as racists.) The solution is not socialism, seen as another failed liberal idea, but nationalism, the natural order of mankind.

It's the substitute teacher theory of society. There was once a real teacher who gave rules the class respected and had the kids sitting straight up, and everyone stayed in school. Now the liberals have fired the old teachers and brought in the substitutes—the liberals *are* the substitutes—and the kids are doing anything they like: throwing paper and making dirty drawings and gossiping in the back of the class. Chaos, as third graders learn, is the natural consequence of the loss of authority. The church, organized religion, parental authority, the stable straight nuclear family, a recognizable homogenous nation with a common cultural inheritance, respect for law itself—all these things have been destroyed or demoralized by liberals, and what's left is empty and inadequate and leaves desperation in its wake: achievement and Amazon shopping for the privileged; lifelong hopelessness and opioid death for the rest. Meaningful order rests on authority. The liberal idea that order is ever mutable or emergent in some mysterious way is just a pious lie intended to cover up liberal hedonism. If we don't have stable authority, the right-wing critique insists, we'll do bad things. The subtler argument adds: if we don't have stable authority, we also won't be able to experience the good ones. Chaos is the enemy of pleasure, too.

These more extreme authoritarian attacks on liberalism come in three basic kinds. Let's call their believers for simplicity's sake—and with the obvious understanding that they cross over and hybridize in many intricate ways—triumphalist authoritarians, theological authoritarians, and tragic authoritarians. The first attack liberal weakness; the second, liberal materialism; the last, liberal hubris.

Triumphalists offer the most familiar kind of right-wing authoritarianism, so much that we often just identify it as what right-wing authoritarianism is. It's based on the belief that the most crucial dimension in life is weakness and strength, and that liberals are incurably *weak*. They are too concerned with an empathetic understanding of their enemies to grasp the permanent rules of power. They make bad bargains with our enemies and allow luxury to undermine their virtue. (One of the originalities of the current vein of triumphalist authoritarianism, from Berlusconi to Trump, is that its boss men tend to be exemplars of decadent luxury rather than critics of it.)

An exaggerated reverence for the military is the triumphalist tough guy's signature—exaggerated because it rarely has much to do with the genuine preoccupations of soldiers and officers, who want more money, more planning, and not so many parades. The tough guys in power usually like to watch, salute, and be saluted more than they like to understand what soldiers actually do.

Above all, triumphalist authoritarians insist that the organizing force in life is the nation—the people, the clan, the *volk*, the privileged ethnic group, our tribe. The constitutional conservative is a patriot, devoted to her country. But she feels no sense of victimization in the existence of neighbors with neighborly differences. For the triumphalist authoritarian, the test of our tribe is its dominance over the other tribes. The only real way of judging a society is not in terms of its culture or even its prosperity but simply in terms of its power. A country could be rich, free—and humiliated. That's *far* worse than being impoverished and proud.

The ideology of authoritarian triumphalism is *always* hostile to what liberals call the rule of law. Triumphalists truly don't believe in equality of treatment or in fair play. They believe in domination—whoever wins, rules. Get your opponents before they get you. This is why, historically, triumphalist tough guys hate liberalism and liberals far more than they hate the other kinds of authoritarianism. (Solzhenitsyn wrote once, with uncanny insight, that the only man Stalin ever trusted was Hitler—certainly Stalin's disbelief and shock when Hitler predictably betrayed him in 1941 seems to suggest that this was so.)

❧

At this point, it's conventional to put in a few warning words about the *causes* of the recent rise of populism and gangster-style authoritarianism in Europe and America. I've tried to outline a few in talking about what happened to Akron. But the simpler and scarier and more important truth is that one or other kind of triumphalist authoritarianism has been the default condition of government for almost all of human history. A king or boss or chieftain comes to power through success in war, or inherits power from some ancestor who won his war, or finds a demagogue's way to power. This is not a special feature of one era or another. Strongman politics and boss-man rule, in simplest form, is the story of mankind. So rather than search for the special circumstances that make it rise (economic anxiety? racial prejudice?), we should accept the truth that it can *always* rise, that the lure of a closed authoritarian society is one permanently present in human affairs, and that the real question is not what makes it happen but what, for brief periods of historical time, has *kept* it from happening.

What is striking, and frightening, about tough-guy triumphalism is how crude it can be and still succeed—unattached to a traditionally charismatic leader, a figure of strength, dash, and daring, of military accomplishment. (As Philip Roth pointed out toward the end of his life, Charles Lindbergh was, at least, a genuine hero, while Donald Trump is not even a competent businessman.) Many great minds in the twentieth century tried to explain the rise and hold of the authoritarian leader. But in retrospect, what is most striking is not the strength of his ideology but the disproportion between his intelligence and its evil. One of the things that makes for false reassurance in the liberal mind about triumphalist authoritarianism is how paltry its avatars can seem and how ridiculous and trivial their guiding ideas so often are. It's all half-witted tweets and Berlusconi-style clowning, and who could be a more transparent nothing than Nigel Farage?

So, I will now do something that you are not supposed to do. I will mention Hitler and the Nazis. We are told to avoid ever citing Hitler and often referred to Godwin's law, which insists that sooner or later all Internet debate will degrade into somebody calling somebody else a Nazi—a truth that has in turn been degraded into the insistence that you should never mention Nazis in a debate. (Attorney Mike Godwin himself disavows *that* idea.) We might go further: we should *always* cite Hitler and continually reinspect the story of the rise of Nazism not because every right-wing authoritarian resembles him but because without looking hard and often—without *remembering*—how it was that someone so obviously second rate could take over a modern nation and lead it, and the world, to catastrophe, we will not be able to combat the lesser strains of the pathogen either. Plagues begin with rats and fleas. We need to keep an eye on them.

Many people will tell you that Hitler had grandiose plans for world conquest. In truth, anyone who has sat down to read Adolf Hitler's *Mein Kampf* will be startled to find that it is not a plan of action so much as a survey of grievances. Hitler, whom we suspect of being an embittered, envious, traumatized loser, presents himself as an embittered, envious, traumatized loser. His resentments are ever present. His father was dense, mean, unforgiving, and opaque; art schools turned him down again and again. The petty rancor and unassuaged disappointments burn on every page, in ways one would think more demoralizing than inspiring to potential followers.

Yet this pervasive sense of resentment clearly vibrated with those who themselves know resentment as a primary emotion. Creepy and miserable and uninspiring as the book seems to any reader now, its theme of having been dissed and disrespected by the elite and left to suffer every indignity of life resonated with an entire social class in Germany after World War I. Even Hitler's Jew hating bears the traces of personal rancor as much as of a "scientific" or racial ideology. (It's telling that his anti-Semitism in *Mein Kampf* is entangled with his Francophobia. The Jews are like the French; they are, in plain English, the people whose parents help them get to go to art school.)

Triumphalist authoritarianism is invariably rooted not in an actual program of national renewal but in a raw sense of humiliation, even if the humiliations can often seem, in retrospect, tiny. The fear of mockery and of being laughed at was so strong in Hitler that it still filled his speeches as late as the moment of maximal power when he launched the Second World War. The Jews and the English are laughing at me, and they won't be allowed to laugh for long! Minor failures, small rejections—being mocked at a banquet or rejected by an art school—make for vast visions of revenge. Some horrible things happen because of big ideas, but some equally horrible things happen because of small humiliations.

The second kind of authoritarianism is less powerful in contemporary practice but far more formidable intellectually. We can call it theological or sometimes theistic authoritarianism. Its practitioners say that yes, we need authority, but authority shouldn't come from human beings. The

great leader is a false prophet. What we need is the authority and glory of God. If we recognize the truth of religion,
whether of Christianity or Islam or another, our problems
are solved. We don't have to accept the arguments in the
agora, nor do we have to sort through potential strongmen,
except inasmuch as they are men of faith. We know how to
organize our society and conduct ourselves because God
has told us what to do through his revelations. Of all the
kinds of order there are in the universe, divine order is the
most beautiful and most essential. To act in indifference to
it is not merely bad policy but horrible arrogance, the arrogance of subjects imagining themselves as rulers.

Theological authoritarians hate liberalism not because
liberals are weak but because they seem so *strong*, so arrogant and complacent in their denial of divine truth. Even
if liberals are individually religious, they are still devotees
of the neutral liberal state, which treats God and his blas-
phemers alike, a daily affront to faith. What's more, the
most important values that liberalism claims—compassion,
sympathy, kindness—are in fact borrowed, if not stolen,
from religion. These are Christian (or Talmudic or Koranic)
values, imported into liberal doctrine as the only means to
keep its fatuous materialism from being too evident. The religious take these values solidly on faith; liberals take them
frivolously, on loan. Liberalism lacks a sense of revelation,
and since human beings work by revelation rather than by
reason, it will always be inadequate to our condition. Liberalism is hedonistic in its rejection of any value larger than
material pleasure, and nihilistic in its rejection of any hope
for an afterlife larger than being able to pass one's debts on
to one's children.

Organized religion in America has, on the whole, come to terms, however reluctantly, with liberal democracy. So much so that we tend to forget how hard it fought against it and for how long. The Roman Catholic Church, in part because its power and dogma are uniquely centralized, led this fight throughout the nineteenth century, insisting that liberal ideas—freedom of the press, of speech, a pluralism of parties, much less of creeds—were anathema. Even the Church of England, which now seems to us all vicars and do-gooding liberal causes, was perceived as one of the chief enemies of the movement for women's suffrage: the suffragettes burned down parish churches and bombed Westminster Abbey.

Theological authoritarianism in actual power today is largely confined to the Muslim world. Iran, for instance, is ruled this way. But as a set of ideas—as a kind of higher calling—it remains potent and present, inflecting the discourse and practice of both constitutional conservatives and, more opportunistically, the triumphalist authoritarians.

Yet there is a more than honorable tradition of theological authoritarianism, of religious-based antiliberalism, that need not bend toward Iran or the Inquisition. Consider, instead, the most attractive and seductive model of theological authoritarianism, as we find it in the works of the best religious writers of the past century. The early twentieth-century English—and latterly Roman Catholic—writer and lecturer G. K. Chesterton was one of the most original, and by far the wittiest, of the religious dissidents from the liberal imagination. Dissatisfied with a merely parliamentary model of life, he put together a potent and charming mix of neomedievalism and Catholic nostalgia and described a purer world of heightened numinous feeling than that of the materialism he saw all around him in Edwardian England. We know from our own experience that the things that inspire us are not, so to speak, waiting in lines at a voting booth but spontaneous moments of exaltation and illumination. To try and find meaning in projects of dutiful reform can seem comical. Earnest well-meaning liberals might obsess on their latest cause—around 1900 it was antivivisection or vegetarianism while nowadays the same kind of people would be obsessed with gender stereotypes or, well, vegetarianism (not everything changes)—but while pursuing their reforms completely miss the exalted spark and mystery of life. The reasonable life is limited and drained of color; only the unreasonable one opens up a crack of light to eternity.

"Reason is always a kind of brute force," Chesterton wrote, in one of his matchless aphorisms. "Those who appeal to the head rather than the heart, however pallid and polite, are necessarily men of violence. We speak of 'touching' a man's heart, but we can do nothing to his head but hit it." Elsewhere he offered the clearest statement of the theological authoritarian's complaint: "Men can agree on the fact that the earth goes around the sun. But then it does not matter a dump whether the earth goes around the sun or the Pleiades. But men cannot agree about morals: sex, property, individual rights, fixity and contracts, patriotism, suicide, public habits of health—these are exactly the things that men tend to fight about. And these are exactly the things that must be settled somehow on strict principles. Study each of them, and you will find each of them works back certainly to a philosophy, probably to a religion."

Without authority derived ultimately from God, we have a mere shouting match of relativism. Without divinely established order, we have anarchy.

Though not necessarily embracing authoritarian rule, this more intelligent strain of religious dissent from liberal norms does insist that the undue hopes liberalism invests in programs of reason and reform are an inadequate measure to the actual range of human longing. Nobody on their deathbed stopped to think about the glory of single-payer health insurance, even if single-payer health insurance was making their last days better. The realm of affairs in which questions of government, good and bad, can speak to us is extremely limited.

What's curious about the books in this God-minded tradition—the Notre Dame political scientist Patrick Deneen has recently produced an impassioned and influential one called, bluntly, *Why Liberalism Failed*—is that, though they're always written ostensibly in response to a very specific circumstance (the dire spiritual condition of France in 1905, the moral crisis of America in 2018), they always say *exactly* the same things and propose exactly the same cure. Chesterton was an inspired aphorist, while Deneen writes in a version of American academese. But one could wholly subsume one critique into the other. Though the illness they announce is always new and will be fatal if not treated, the prescription never changes. It is always, essentially: "Gimme that old-time religion, especially the kind with a high white hat."

The continuous complaint is that liberalism is atomizing. Liberalism honors the individual before the divine. Liberalism is inherently and duplicitously and incurably divided against itself: it pretends to honor freedom and liberty and instead enforces enslavement to the market and to material pleasure. You sign away your soul for one-click shopping.

For Deneen, the reigning "liberalocracy" of our time glorifies the individual pursuit of pleasure and power to an insane degree, creating a tiny elite of the empowered and a vast populace of the alienated. "The liberalocratic family rests upon loose generational ties, portable credentials, the inheritance of fungible wealth, and the promise of mobility." (You might say that that, indeed, sounds more or less like our family, aside from all that inherited wealth. Inheritance aside—a big aside—it's really *not* so far from what we were observing about ourselves at that Persian restaurant in Manhattan.)

Liberalism proposes a world of such narrow self-fulfillment that it naturally alienates all but the small group of self-seekers it benefits, and even they are mostly miserable. If we look at the important liberal thinkers, this line of attack claims, we find a straight line between their exhortation to "self-realization" and the dispensation of ever-coarser and merely material pleasure. John Stuart Mill's instruction to realize oneself fully was merely a "lifestyle liberalism," and his direction to seek self-fulfillment a direct path to Pornhub. Once you eliminate fixed divine standards, you have nothing but opportunism, hedonism, and anarchy. A few very smart and very shrewd people may do well in such an unmoored world, but the great mass of mankind are devastated by it. For every kid who advances to an Ivy League university and joins the liberalocracy, there are a hundred affected, in one way or another, by the opioid epidemic. Populism becomes an understandable reaction against this liberal destruction of communities that once looked high to heaven or deep into sacred texts for their idea of order.

Obviously, like all moralists, the Catholic moralist flourishes by not looking too closely at the people he's moralizing over, who tend to have far more complicated moral consciousnesses than this account allows. Yet the core of the complaint is significant—seeing this bigger picture helps us choose sides not just in obvious moral controversies like abortion but (Deneen is blunt about this) against such other fruits of the liberal order as gay marriage and premarital sex and even the widespread use of contraception, which makes premarital sex possible. The rage is far too frequent to dismiss. Liberalism, we are told, in different voices but always in nearly the same words, succeeds only in a world "stripped of custom, and the kinds of institutions that transmitted cultural norms, habituated responsibility, and cultivated ordinary virtues." That kind of success should only be called failure.

Nor, it should be said, does this religious-minded critique necessarily only emerge from the right. The contemporary Canadian philosopher Charles Taylor, though as far from right wing in his politics as it is possible to imagine—he ran several times for the Parliament of Canada as a social democrat in the New Democratic Party—is the most cogent critic of the militant secularism of liberalism and of the inability of mere procedural, individualist hedonism to fulfill our need for shared meaning. (I attended the university, McGill in Montreal, to which he was an ornament, and his many children, presumably products of Catholic virtue, often intermingled with my many siblings, products of Jewish secularism.)

A liberal might say that to know who I am is, as with a musical comedy hero in act one, to know what I *want*— what I'm driven toward, what I desire. Taylor's point is that to know who I really am is to know *where* I am—how I'm placed within a social context that I didn't make and can't control. "My identity is defined by the commitments and identifications which provide the frame or horizon within which I can try to determine from case to case what is good, or valuable, or what ought to be done, or what I endorse or oppose." Liberalism, in this different view, drives us forward to maximize our utility. "It's not just that people sacrifice their love relationships, and the care of their children, to pursue their careers. Something like this has perhaps always existed. The point is that today many people feel *called* to do this, feel they ought to do this, feel their lives would be somehow wasted or unfulfilled if they didn't do it." We all feel, Taylor tells us, "profound malaise at the idea that the sources of benevolence should be just enlightened self-interest, or simply feelings of sympathy. This seemed to neglect altogether the human power of self-transcendence, the capacity to go beyond self-related desire altogether and follow a higher aspiration."

Even in Taylor's more progressive revolt against liberal secularism, the need for some permanent horizon of fulfillment larger than the temporary social agreement of individuals to buy and sell one another things, including things like university degrees, is always felt. The good things in life are beautiful and can be bought, but the best things in life are free and freely given. Liberal secularism drains the world of meaning by reducing our desire for the highest and the most to a craving merely for *more*.

This more philosophical edge of the religious rejection of liberalism leads us finally to a less visible but in its way more profound right-wing creed, not necessarily theistic or even religious, which we can call tragic authoritarianism. It is the authoritarianism of one of my intellectual heroes, a man we've already encountered and who I love: the eighteenth-century journalist and philosopher, Samuel Johnson. He thought that life was too sad to be cured by politics. Even good government ended in death. It is also a form of the attack on liberalism one finds as well in the so-called Straussians, followers of the Jewish American classical philosopher Leo Strauss. To this type, the past is not a place to be outstripped and discarded, surpassed and condescended to. The past is in a real sense the only place we have.

The tragic authoritarian's chief enemy is not liberal secularism as such but liberal *progressivism*. Tragic authoritarians think that liberalism is neither too soft nor too hard but too blinkered and self-satisfied. Liberalism is guilty of enormous hubris. To rest our hopes in material betterment, or social advancement, or even egalitarian reform is ridiculous. Our lives are filled with loss and illness and misery and sickness and even when improved by reform end in the same shared mortality. The central human issues were as evident to the ancients as to us, and they argued about them more honestly. Liberalism scoffs at a past it scarcely understands. Given the brevity of our lives and the uncertainty of our accomplishments, we can hardly believe that even a better sewer will help very much. That's why Dr. Johnson called one of his poems "The Vanity of Human Wishes." Where we need to invest ourselves is not in pointless programs of material betterment but in training in self-recognition.

This is not a position that many working politicians would subscribe to or even understand. But it helps explain the oft-remarked *silence* of some conservative intellectuals about authoritarian leaders—and their search for a "heroic" politics outside the liberal dispensation. Martin Heidegger has been attacked savagely for having crossed over and joined the Nazi Party in the early thirties. A close reader of Heidegger, which I am not, insists that while it is a mistake to see a connection between his philosophical writings and Nazism, it is true that his acute sense of the daily crisis of existence made him impatient with normal parliamentary politics and their life-defying anesthesia.

Triumphal authoritarianism, particularly in America, is often an anti-intellectual movement—those damned elites with their damned *ideas*. But when it is allied to this larger tragic sense of limits foolishly ignored, particularly of the limits of reason, it can become intellectually serious, even formidable.

While in America the new right, or alt-right, has a largely schoolboy sniggering quality, in recent years an efflorescence of literature from the New Right in Europe has married an old antirationalist and tragic, fatalist strain in European philosophy with a vengeful hatred of contemporary liberalism. The lines of this kind of reasoning run right from Heidegger and the other antirational philosophers of the early part of the twentieth century to such thinkers as Aleksandr Dugin, the house philosopher of the Putin regime, even known as Putin's brain. (No one has been named, so far, as Trump's.)

The ferocity of the complaint derives not just from Heidegger but from such uncompromising earlier right-wing thinkers as Julius Evola, who was too far right in too completely crazy a way even for the Nazis. Alain de Benoist, the leader of the New Right in France, in his manifesto for the movement, sums up the general critique with chilling clarity. There's the clan basis of community: "Communities are constituted and maintain themselves on the basis of who belongs to them. Membership is all that is required. There is a vertical reciprocity of rights and duties, contributions and distributions, obedience and assistance, and a horizontal reciprocity of gifts, fraternity, friendship, and love." And when he says that "membership is all that is required," he states the essential clan belief: you don't have to earn your place by passing some meritocratic test. Your existence as "one of us" makes you at home here. De Benoist writes that the "New Right affirms the primacy of differences, which are neither transitory features leading to some higher form of unity, nor incidental aspects of private life. Rather, these differences are the very substance of social life. They can be native (ethnic, linguistic), but also political." Ethnic differences, from country to country and clan to clan, are not to be suppressed but privileged, celebrated. An ideal European union would not be between countries that have been anesthetized by liberal "universalism" but rather between nations that have learned to respect one another's sharply different ethnic, racial, religious, and cultural identities. Liberal reason, in this view, is the perpetual enemy of community. Liberals use reason to reason you out of your identity.

Here, too, artists bring more insight than polemicists. Some version of de Benoist's critique is also at the core of the beliefs of the hugely popular (and scandalous) French novelist Michel Houellebecq, surely the writer of the moment in Europe, if anyone is. In the novel that made him famous, *Les Particles Élémenataires*, Houellebecq proposed that a society with an unchecked devotion both to liberalism in the economic sense and libertinism in the erotic sense would eventually lead to one of more or less compulsory oscillation between, well, fucking and finance, where bankers would literally break their backs in the act of having sex for the hundredth time that day. The satire seemed ridiculously heavy-handed and overwrought—and then there appeared Dominique Strauss-Kahn, the actual head of the International Monetary Fund and a man of such compulsive sexual appetite that he turned out, in the brief time between dining with his daughter and boarding a plane, to have budgeted fifteen minutes for sex with a total stranger. Only Houellebecq could, so to speak, have preimagined DSK.

Houellebecq's most recent (and most infamous) novel, *Submission*, about an Islamic takeover of France, is supposedly an anti-Islamic warning story. Yet in fact it is an admiring account of Islamic militancy, seen as a plausible alternative to the vitiated forms of modern liberalism. *All* the most eloquent spokesmen in the book are religious minded and in favor of theocracy. The struggle of the twentieth century, the narrator explains, was between two failed humanisms—the hard humanism of communism and the soft humanism of liberal capitalism, each in its way "horribly reductive."

Houellebecq is a satirist and more complicated than a too-neat summary suggests. But we shouldn't miss that he has captured a strong and intelligent vein of feeling about liberalism today. The sense of the loss of identity, faith, of meaning itself caused by liberalism is clearly as powerful a sentiment as exists in Europe. This is the far edge of the right-wing assault—but history shows that the far edge has a way of becoming the cutting edge much sooner than anyone might think.

We may think of it as a revolt against reason, but what we're living through is a revolt against *liberal* reason, against a kind of reason that reduces all difference to a "brand" and all blood ties to an archaic hoax and all difference to an archaic difficulty. In this view, the great universalist projects of late twentieth-century liberalism—the European Union, for instance—are classic instances of the folly of liberal reason. They substitute absurdly grandiose abstract ideas for the tragic wisdom of lived experience and end by offering their citizens nothing to live by or with except a currency—and in this case, a currency with a nihilistic imagery of nothingness on its face, all those euro bills without national heroes and heroines to decorate them, just nameless bridges leading nowhere.

⚜

What can the liberal say in response to all of these assaults?

First, that the broader communitarian assault on liberalism depends on a very false picture of what liberals have ever believed, or what liberals in power have, for good or ill, actually done. The idea that liberalism is narrowly devoted only to individual rights and the pursuit of selfish material well-being is a cartoon with little connection to liberal ideas or practices.

If we look at all the classic liberal texts and, more important, the actual historical political practices of liberalism, we see immediately that all have a powerful idea of collectivity and community at their heart. Adam Smith is not Ayn Rand. Smith believes that the sympathy of a community, escaping from fearful clan feuds, is the necessary prelude to free-market exchanges. As Habermas and Putnam have each in their different ways shown us, liberal *political* practices rest on liberal *social* practices—the Declaration of the Rights of Man begins with a conversation in a café, and local democracy has a better chance of triumphing in Italy when amateur opera groups sing out first.

The great liberal thinkers whose shared arc I've been trying to describe all began by reflecting on relationships, on what happens when people meet people and what obligations they have to each other. Montaigne brooding on compassion was not brooding on the inner life alone; he was thinking about what happened to animals when men went in groups to hunt them and what happened to the men's minds after they killed the animals. John Stuart Mill and Harriet Taylor were not opposed to the duties of family life. Just the opposite: they paused from starting one of their own because they wanted to show respect for the family life Taylor already had. They just thought that family life ought to be fairer to everyone in the family. What's called liberal individualism always emerges from an assumed background of connectedness.

More concretely, the great liberal politicians of the mid-nineteenth century who helped turn liberalism from an ancient idea of generosity and cultivation into an effective political practice were all rooted in the project of reinforcing common bonds. The liberal revolutions of that era were *unifying* revolutions, bringing together different ethnic groups under the common umbrella of one nation. We think of modern nationalism as a divisive poison, but in the nineteenth century, liberal nationalism was inherently patriotic in the modern sense, a way of reaching *past* divides among people to create nations—out of many, one.

That kind of liberalism was supremely preoccupied with building coherent communities across ethnic lines. A moving, though in America, little-known example occurred in 1849 when Robert Baldwin, the Protestant leader of Upper Canada, today's Ontario, and Louis-Hippolyte LaFontaine, the leader of the almost exclusively Catholic Quebec, then called Lower Canada, joined together against an anti-Catholic mob in Montreal, for both national unity and liberal rights. They had every reason to break apart into two warring tribes, but Lafontaine and Baldwin defied the rioting English-speaking crowd, standing with one another to demonstrate that national unity was possible on a biethnic and even religious basis. On the basis of that nonviolent but stoically determined demonstration, the Canadian nation was born. Lafontaine wrote beautifully that "[Canada] is our homeland, as it should be the adopted homeland of the different populations that come from the diverse parts of the globe. . . . Their children should be, like us, and above all, Canadians. In addition to social equality, we need political liberty. Without it, we will have no future; without it, our needs cannot be satisfied. . . . These values are stronger than laws, and nothing we know of will weaken them."

Social equality and political liberty—one depends on the other. Canada has been called the model liberal nation and certainly depends for its persistence on a neutral liberal state. It is sometimes surprising for even a bilingual Canadian like me to see bilingual notices on every project that involves the federal government, even in places where there are vanishingly few French speakers. But the point is not to promote neutrality as a virtue in itself. Rather, these practices emerge out of the knowledge of how many passions reign in a nation and from a desire to allow them to simmer without burning the house down.

The name of Léon Gambetta is one not widely known outside France, but he, too, was a great founding liberal who understood that unity, not mere coalition, was a Republican cause. The establishment of the Paris Commune in 1871 led to the bloodiest possible confrontation between reactionary royalists and radical communists. Both sides committed atrocities, the right's bloodier than the left's because they had more guns and opportunities. The cleavage in French society seemed absolute, violent, and fatal.

Yet even in that moment, it was not necessary to see France's future in such a permanently polarized and self-annihilating manner. Gambetta, an ordinary grocer's son, fled the Prussian siege of Paris in a balloon—an honest-to-god balloon—and, on his return, eventually came to captain a political grouping that called itself the Opportunist Republicans. Surely no political movement in history has ever borne a less inspiring name, but its central insight was sound: that the future of the left lay with coalitions of different estates, petty bourgeois and peasantry and proletariat mixed up, not with a commune representing only one and committed to itself. Gambetta convinced the responsible left to embrace legislative republicanism single-mindedly, not out of fear but out of wisdom: the only way to maintain a real revolution in increased rights and protections was to recognize that rejecting the legitimacy of the opposition could end only in violence. Jean Jaurès—one of the founders of the French Socialist Party and the greatest left-wing populist hero France has produced—embraced the republic, and all its exhausting parliamentary maneuverings, because he understood the unimaginable costs that renewed civic warfare would bring. The right had to be opposed; it could not be eliminated.

It was the world that the radical republicans in France built painfully out of the ruins of the Paris Commune that Manet and his followers depicted in some of the most moving images of muted domestic—and explosive urban—joy that have ever been painted. As the impressionists remind us, the neutral state, the plural city, that liberalism constructs is never neutral emotionally. It shines.

❧

While the creation of community is central to the liberal ideal, the conservative dream of clan identity is itself a kind of unicorn. Nations and tribes are not the same, and clans are not communities. The punchline to the story of the big clan at the next table at that Persian restaurant was that the big Armenian clan we had envied and admired was actually the family of Vartan Gregorian, the former president of Brown. What looked from across the room like a purer and more uncorrupted clan world out there was actually as cosmopolitan as our own.

That's a comically extreme and very local Manhattan instance. But whenever we examine supposedly organic communities, they turn out to be more complicated than they look—and more cautionary than right-wing communitarians believe. As escapees tell us, these communities can be severely limiting. (*Hillbilly Elegy* was written by someone who had gotten far away, and Chrissie Hynde's memories of Akron were written, safely, far from Ohio.)

The appeal to the lost organic community, either in its rigorous Spartan militarism or a more swooning medievalist faith, is so overwhelming that it recurs ceaselessly. In ancient Athens, clan identity and the closed society of Sparta were appealing to aristocrats fed up with messy democracy, and then in the nineteenth century the dream of a relentlessly high-minded (and homoerotic) Athens was often appealing to English aristocrats fed up with another messy encroaching popular democracy of their own. We always want that other fixed and stable place. (Aesthetes, as a rule, can live only in an open society while dreaming always of a closed one.)

But we can state, categorically and certainly, that no such good place exists or has ever existed—it is a country populated entirely by unicorns. Invariably, the whole notion that there is an uncorrupted clan or faith world out there is false. Whenever we go to actually examine that more organic society that liberalism has allegedly annihilated, it always turns out to be not organic at all, but as uncomfortably divided as our own and with more murderous rules of social exclusion. (As today the America of the fifties is held up for admiration and nostalgic envy, looking past the brutality toward black people and the still subjugated state of women and the oppression of homosexuals.)

Whenever you look at a group with secure clan identity, there's always conformity and a radical course of culling out those who don't belong. The idea of an organic, traditional, closed community is unreal because it takes the inevitable fact of human variation and tries to liquidate it. It's not as though such communities once predominated and were then killed off by modern liberalism. Ancient and medieval cities could often achieve a rich practice of coexistence. In Jerusalem around 1000, as a recent show at the Metropolitan Museum showed beautifully, a thriving mix of trade and commerce among Jews and Christians and Muslims went on more than fitfully. (A single object, the so-called Hedwig beaker, showed charmingly how this entanglement can still befuddle historians. Was this little object, found in Germany, European glass emulating an Islamic style, or Islamic glass made for a European market?) It's not that hard to find a practice of cosmopolitanism, even in the things that hold our daily wine: Christian gospels written in Arabic hands, Hebrew inscriptions on Islamic astrolabes, above all the confounding of markets and merchandise. The whole end of liberalism is to turn the human habit of coexistence into a principle of pluralism, one that mediates crises between communities instead of surrendering to mutual murder among them. Yet this all ended in massacre and counter-massacre.

Nor does any actual image of a possible religious state emerge from the religious right because no one actually wants to create it. The modern semitheocracies that have been established—either aggressively as in Iran, or more dully in Francoist Spain, or even in a church-dominated state like post independence Ireland—have been uninspiring, to put it mildly. Theological authoritarianism and antiliberalism in practice is at best dreary and life negating (and, of course, its Catholic variant marked by an unusual frequency of child rape by the moral leaders). And so, the more flexible or alert religious authoritarians usually grumblingly insist that they accept or even genuflect to liberal institutions—free speech, fair elections, the equality of women, and the rest—even as they go on hating the liberalism that uniquely brought those institutions into existence.

This is, I think, the central liberal reply to the communitarian complaint as it comes at us from conservative politicians and philosophers: liberalism actually builds and reinforces common bonds as much as any political practice can. Indeed, it depends on them. But it also recognizes the truth that a closed or clan or ethnic society invariably either can't be realized, or that, if we try to realize it, doing so involves coercion on a scale that makes the enforced assertion of a common identity far crueler than its erasure. There are no "people like us." As soon as we are surrounded by people like us, we start seeing how much unlike us some of them are, and the cycle of exclusion and excommunication begins again.

The liberal also knows that even the most fixed and belligerent categories of identity turn out to be mutable. We can see how much the concept of "white people" has expanded to include Jews and Irish Catholics, who were at various recent points seen as mortal *enemies* of "whiteness," not merely not white but antiwhite. The same process can happen in reverse: the alt-right in America wants to once again excommunicate Jews from their recently acquired whiteness, and we have already seen how the Trump administration is de-Americanizing the Hispanics, who a brief while ago were seen as the bellwether of new Americanness. The excommunications among the people-like-us crowd never end.

⁓⁂⁓

What of the more specific assaults on liberal institutions? The liberal argument against triumphal authoritarianism involves truths about history; with theological authoritarianism, truths about pluralism; and with the tragic kind, truths about, well, truth.

The first argument is an argument from experience. Those societies that glorify militarism almost invariably lose wars. Since everything depends on the boss man's favor, such societies are not accidentally but inherently corrupt and invariably end up promoting only yes-men and yes-women. Only mediocrity rises, because only mediocrity can feign loyalty that well.

The historical truth is that the "weaknesses" of liberalism have always been imaginary. In almost every confrontation between open liberal societies and closed authoritarian ones, the liberal state has triumphed. In each case, prior to the conflict, or during it, the liberal state was described, usually by right-wingers within it, as fatally weak, ruined by permissiveness, undermined by dissent, distracted by material pleasure, and lacking the discipline and order and readiness for self-sacrifice that a confrontation with the ordered and regimented enemy demanded. It was too weak (and, often, too feminine) to fight. This was true in the American Civil War, true in the Second World War, true in the Cold War—yet in each case, the open pluralist society triumphed over the closed one by the combined force of cultural example and technological advance.

Or consider the more recent war on terror, during which it was (and still is, in some quarters) repeated, again and again, that Islamic terrorists had a militant faith, a self-reliance, discipline, and belief that mere liberal cities like New York lacked. This is a variant of Houellebecq's point in *Submission*. Eighteen years after 9/11, the liberal city has repaired and renewed itself, while the jihadists look weaker, as a "moral" force, than they ever have. They seem still capable of killing but hardly capable of inspiring.

This may not *always* happen. A liberal state can lose a war. (America lost to North Vietnam.) But, as a horse-racing tout would say, that's the form—and there is no reason to bet against the form. An authoritarian state, bending to the will of a strongman, invariably becomes corrupt and stagnant. The great liberal philosopher Karl Popper long ago pointed out that in a closed or authoritarian society it is also almost impossible for there to be the rich practice of any science, or any real growth of knowledge, since knowledge depends on the free play of criticism—the one thing such authoritarian societies can't indulge. It is not an accident that long periods of theocratic rule or of gangster government fossilize all thought. (Nor that dissidence tends to rise from the reluctantly protected scientific elite, as with Andrei Sakharov in the old Soviet Union.)

It is hard to find successful authoritarian societies, even if we mean by success merely that the state provides a more or less satisfying life for more or less most of its people. If you placed medieval France alongside contemporary France, there's no doubt about which way the refugees would be running. Knowledge won't grow in such strongman societies, and even the simplest kinds of prosperity are always endangered by corruption and clan-centered dealings. There's nothing weaker than a strongman state, even when there's nothing louder than the strongman.

To the theological kind, the classic liberal reproach has been similar. Secularism may be a sin, but there has been no place so safe to make this complaint as the secularized talking shops of liberal societies, where even God can compete with God.

For the trouble with turning to God is that there are just too many gods. As a historical fact, tolerance is not an imposition of liberalism or of the Enlightenment to declaw the church. It began instead before the Enlightenment, in the seventeenth century, at the end of exhausting periods of religious warfare, as a kind of pact between competing churches. Tolerance is a treaty among faiths more than an imposition *on* faith.

I've tried not to write too much about the famous seventeenth- and eighteenth-century English philosophers who helped found the liberal credo, concentrating instead on liberal lives that offer a better guide to living liberal practice. But to read either John Locke or John Milton in their famous writings on tolerance is not to read contract-minded documents pointing out that you can make more money if you have fewer religious wars. It's to see the intrusion of a new emotional value. That value is horror, horror at religious violence. The logic of religious intolerance is on its own terms perfectly lucid: if you think you have unique access to the secrets of the cosmos and eternal life, why *wouldn't* you be intolerant of those who do not subscribe to that truth? What Locke and Milton saw is the huge human cost of that belief. There was just too much cruelty in their century as a result of it. They enjoined a common humility in the face of a Christian God whose ultimate purposes we could never know. Locke in 1689 writes that religious people should only turn to: "arguments; which yet (with their leave) is the only right method of propagating truth. . . . Those that are of another opinion would do well to consider with themselves how pernicious a seed of discord and war, how powerful a provocation to endless hatreds, rapines, and slaughters they thereby furnish unto mankind. No peace and security, no, not so much as common friendship, can ever be established or preserved amongst men so long as this opinion prevails, that dominion is founded in grace and that religion is to be propagated by force of arms."

Locke's point isn't that all ideas are of equivalent value. It's that hatred and rapine and slaughter are bad *in themselves* and that because experience shows these are the consequences of religious intolerance, religious intolerance must be bad too. It is a plea for peace, not a neutral shrug of indifference to truth. It is, again, the assertion of a new value, not an abstract rule.

Faith has never flourished so freely and variously as it has in the liberal city. On a Friday night in the Brooklyn neighborhood of Williamsburg, to see the range and defiantly distinctive dress of the Hasidim coming to and from their shuls on the streets they share with hipsters and West Indians is deeply moving even to those Jews who view the enclosed lives of the ultraorthodox ultraskeptically. If liberalism is in any sense intolerance then it is hard to see it on the street. What is meant by secularism is usually, simply the proliferation of different religion faiths; a lot can look like nothing to eyes searching for only one.

If what is genuinely wanted is space for faith practices—rather than power for one of them alone—then no societies have opened more doors to the spiritual life than the liberal democracies or offered more shelter for worship. Some liberals are hostile to religion; some are indifferent; some are welcoming; and some are religious themselves. Of the liberal minds we've met so far, some were believers, some freethinkers, while most pursued a spiritual path of their own quiet devising. The greatest English-speaking poet of the mid-twentieth century, W. H. Auden, was a liberal in politics and a sincere and passionate Christian; the greatest critic of the same time, his good friend William Empson, was a liberal in politics and a sincere and passionate polemicist against Christianity.

Anyone who feels the loss of a sacred presence in liberal society is not paying attention. A renewed sense of the sacred is the great theme of modernist art, from Kandinsky to Rothko and beyond. Of the central figures of modern American letters, at least as many are religiously obsessed—J. D. Salinger, John Updike, Jane Smiley—as are hostile to religion. What we have witnessed is not any loss of a sense of the sacred but a loss of sacred authority, a different thing. Now, in the liberal model of faith, the sacred is spread by consent rather than coercion.

Nothing exists to prevent someone from articulating a conservative Christian or Islamic code in public in any of the great democracies. They get articulated all the time. The issues on which Christians particularly tend to rest their case for intolerance and persecution turn out to be, in any sane historical perspective, absurdly tiny—the possibility, for instance, that a fundamentalist baker might be forced to bake a gay cake. (Which is not to say that liberals might not benefit from *not* forcing these tiny cases where they are not absolutely essential to equality of treatment. Open lunch counters are essential to equality. Are open-minded bakers as essential? Liberals should not be fine-print artists; having gotten the big things, they should not sweat the small ones too much.)

One often reads in religious-minded polemics about the "totalitarian" nature of liberalism and the "nihilism" of the liberal ethic. It's perfectly true that liberalism is not neutral and that it has a metaphysics of its own. But this metaphysics is not a weak, surreptitious alternative to that of faith but is rather its knowing opposite. The hidden metaphysics of liberalism is simply that it values debate and hates dogma and accepts doubleness. If you do not want to have your dogma put up for debate, the liberal state will be an uncomfortable place to live within.

For on actual examination the nihilism ascribed to liberalism just means pluralism, and its totalitarianism just means tolerance. Even the supposed loss of secure community is in itself a chimera. In my experience, no orthodox marriage on a Greek island is celebrated with as much solemnity and ceremony combined as is a gay marriage on Fire Island in New York. (Gay marriages tend to be extremely well produced.) Liberalism constitutes countless communities of common feeling. They're just not those of a church or synagogue or mosque. From the devotees who travel to Comic-Con impersonating Chewbacca, to those who travel to Skepticon impersonating Christopher Hitchens, liberalism is full of community. They make friends and lovers along the way—very much in the spirit of medieval pilgrims headed to Canterbury. No, liberalism is dense with community; it simply makes new, non-traditional kinds of community. (For that matter, online communities where fetishist speaks to fellow fetishist are as alive with gossip as any idealized country store. Sexual license may be shallow, but it certainly gets people talking to each other.) The Chestertons and Deneens of the world, insisting that liberalism destroys values, tend to overlook the overwhelming liberal assertion of the primary human value of pluralism because to them pluralism is simply not a value.

Invariably, that is the real complaint of the believer: having lost authority the believers must now submit to the same struggle of contested claims as everyone else. Even if you try to read the theological authoritarians as charitably as possible, you realize that what offends them is not being forced to live *within* moral categories they dislike but being forced to live *around* moral communities not their own—to accept that there are other legitimate ways of pursuing a good life, possessed of an equally rich sense of what we, too, call the sacred, just differently defined. The harm done is simply the harm of seeing other people doing things you happen not to like, and one is "forced" to join in only inasmuch as one is "forced" to live as a citizen among other citizens.

Tolerance is a truce among churches, a nonaggression pact among many gods after centuries of religious warfare. Barriers do exist to the *exclusivity* of any religion; they are the barriers of civic peace. If exclusivity is essential, the liberal responds, then the creed must not be very powerful. If a credo uniquely blessed by God cannot compete and win against other credos, not nearly so blessed, in the open competition of ideas that is the heart of the liberal ethic—then, the liberal replies, the weakness surely resides elsewhere than in the agora that welcomes the argument.

It is certainly true that some of the ideas of liberalism derive from older religious ideas. How could they not? All ideas derive from older ones, as so many Christian ideals derive from pagan philosophical ones. (Darwin got the idea of evolution, though not the evidence for it, from his grandfather.) But few ideas could be more fatuous than that secular ideals are really "just as religious" as religious ideals. The frequent insistence that everyone has a religion, or that liberalism is a religion like any other, is as absurd as saying that a belief in tolerance is the same as a belief in intolerance because both are beliefs, or that a hot bath is the same as a cold bath because both are made of water.

What distinguishes religions from philosophies and points of view and all the other ways people cope with the difficulties of the world—the only reason to use that specific word rather than some other—is that the religious accept the fact of supernatural intervention at some historical moment. The great faiths may have every shade of humane value, from Sufi mysticism to Islamist militancy. But one can't really be a Christian without believing that Jesus was resurrected, or a Muslim without believing that the Qur'an was dictated by an angel, or Jewish without believing in either a creator or a chosen people. When you say, as I would, "I'm Jewish, but I don't believe in either a creator or a chosen people," what you are saying, precisely, is "I am not a religious Jew." There is one set of things that is fairly called religious beliefs, and another set that is fairly called worldviews or philosophies of life; to insist that one is the same as the other is just an imperialist annexation of meaning on the part of the religious (who often can't see past their own religion to recognize other people's beliefs).

Or as Penn Jillette once said, the argument that liberal humanism is a religion like any other is the same as the argument that, since stamp collecting is an obsessive hobby, then *not* stamp collecting must be an obsessive hobby too. You must be contemptuous of people who collect stamps, spend your time excoriating some strange two-penny issue, and rage at night as you look up old issues of rare variants to burn. We can imagine such a person. Such a person would be a comic figure in a parody of religion.

In fact, people who don't collect stamps don't have an alternative passion for not collecting stamps. If you don't love stamps, you don't hate stamps. You just don't care about stamps. Such people are completely content to allow other people to pursue their stamp-collecting obsession without feeling a need for any parallel fanaticism of their own. It seems difficult for people of an authoritarian cast of mind to really accept that there are other people who don't need authority to be happy—just as people who are haunted by mortality are persuaded that everyone else must be too and that no one can live in recognition of their own impending doom and still believe in constructive work and a meaningful life.

John Stuart Mill certainly underwent a spiritual crisis as a young man, which made him unhappy with the colder kinds of rationalism in which he had been instructed by his father. But he *never* turned toward any idea of God, a conception he regarded as fatuous and unimpressive, not to say self-evidently silly. He turned instead toward a larger and more humane idea of what reform might be, not his father's ideal of utilitarian measurement but one that took in Mozart, music, love, and literature. He never stopped thinking that alleviating other people's pain is the first duty of public policy. What liberals have, he thought, is better than a religion. It is a way of life.

Nothing could be further from the truth than the idea that the values of liberalism are simply wanly recycled from religion. Replacing sacred truths with common sympathy and shared sentiments or with self-evident propositions; believing in the fallibility of all human beliefs; insisting on skepticism about all claims; making incremental social improvement and the removal of suffering a higher goal than eternal salvation; placing more emphasis on the well-being of the next generation and on the "horizontal" axis of life than on achieving eternal bliss through the "vertical" one— these distinguishing traits of the liberal temperament are not the traits of any existing religion. They are new ideas.

If anything, the reverse is true: liberal and humanist ideals have been back-projected onto the ancient documents of faith, which are almost always preoccupied, and understandably so, with parables of obedience and tribal right, fidelity and vengeance, punishment and salvation. The Hebrew Bible, obsessed in its day with fanatic dietary restrictions and the rules of animal sacrifice in holy places, is retrospectively turned into a document of universalist, humane measures. And while the idea of radical equality may be implicit in Christianity, *achieving* radical equality, a completely different conception, is a liberal and modern idea. One is accomplished at best as a form of spiritual solidarity, or else in an afterlife or a remote apocalyptic moment (and has always been completely compatible in practice with an authoritarian hierarchy). The other is all sewers and coffeehouses, public works and social sanity, small advances and worldly pleasures, and the welfare of our children, not the terror of our gods.

⁂

Liberals believe that the authoritarian choice between a world with certainty and a world of chaos is a false one. Between anarchy and authority lies argument. Authority is hollow if it is not reinforced with *argument*—actual argument, not the repetition of axioms—and argument is empty if it is not based on evidence and a search for shared facts. That was Locke's antidote to religious warfare: arguing out the rights and wrongs in an open setting. Argument is always the antidote to fanaticism.

Tragic authoritarianism, in turn, will seem to the liberal imagination to be true in its analysis but too despairing in its diagnosis. We need not embrace the frantic rhythms of a revived irrationalism to recognize all the truth that a tragic vision of life contains. We can believe in the importance of ameliorating pain without thinking that every kind of pain can always be ameliorated. We can want a better life for all without thinking that a better life can cure the fact of death.

I think of my friend Katha Pollitt, a fine progressive columnist, who for decades has fought in the pages of the *Nation* magazine for feminism and fairness and particularly for woman's reproductive rights. She is also an even better melancholic poet, and once, in printed conversation, I asked her how she reconciled her progressive politics with the tragic sense of life I find so touching in her poetry. If life is this sad, does it really matter if a Democrat gets elected city council president? She admitted, honestly, that "even if tomorrow America turned into the somewhat idealized Scandinavia that *Nation* readers would love to live in, there would still be the central human predicament. Not just death, decay, the passing of beauty, unrequited love, unrealized ambitions and all that, but the poor fit between human consciousness, and, well, I don't exactly know what to call it—*reality*? We want life to have more meaning than it actually possesses—that is the human tragedy, or maybe I should say tragicomedy."

Even the most compassionate program of egalitarian reform inevitably ends up against the limits of being human. We can't make men and women live forever; we can't make the people they love love them back. We can't cure loneliness, and we can't make good dogs go to heaven. Willie Nelson once said in my hearing, though not I think for the first time—I was writing a profile of him—that "99 percent of the world's lovers are not with their first choice, and that's what makes the jukebox play." Liberal prosperity may buy you an extra beer, but it can't change the set list on the juke box.

One of the values of having a faith in reason is exactly that it shows you the shape and outline of all that can't be reasoned. A large part of human life is subject to irrational wishes and desires that can't be reformed away. "The sleep of reason begets monsters," Goya told us, a romantic motto. Liberals may rightly refuse to claim parentage of the monsters of unreason, but we have to take responsibility for them. They must be managed, for they can rarely be mastered. A liberalism that underrates the human need for stable order and symbolic identity and looks past the common truth of mortality too exclusively toward the horizon of mere market-bound materialism is one that will soon become a unicorn itself.

CHAPTER THREE

WHY THE LEFT HATES
LIBERALISM

THE RIGHT-WING critique or assault on liberalism is chiefly an attack on its undue faith in *reason*. Reason is not enough to live by. Our common life was never made to a rational recipe. Nations, peoples—true nations, true peoples—the great reactionaries tell us, can only be held together by will, shared identity, the assertion of raw power, and the presence of pure faith, not by measured argument. Right-wing antiliberal movements effectively weaponize that belief: Fatherland and Country, Make America Great Again, Forward, Italy! The politics of national grandeur, I hope I've made clear, need not *only* be the province of gangsters and clowns and crooks and con men: de Gaulle's career shows us that, and so does Disraeli's. But they all too often are. In their ugliest faces and phases—and they have a way of getting very ugly very quickly—they depend on visions of revenge and vengeance and domination and conquest or reconquest.

The left-wing critique of liberalism is chiefly an attack on liberal faith in *reform*. Only revolutionary change can bring justice and equality to a criminally unjust world. This assault on liberalism comes from a very different place, at once closer and much further away. Closer because many of the values the left holds—a faith that the future can be better than the past and a confidence that spiritual improvements depend on material ones, that we have to be well fed before we can be high minded—are ones that liberals share. Further away because the leftist assault on tradition and the past tends to be more breathtakingly absolute than the traditionalist authoritarian right can dream of or desire. Year Zero, the idea of beginning time itself over and starting the calendar anew, is a Jacobin concept—a founding radical concept.

In imagining the left critique, I think of the moment when your brother, Luke, was reading about the genocide in the Belgian Congo for school. I was at that same moment in the middle of reading and reviewing one more book about the Holocaust—Timothy Snyder's fine, controversial account of the "bloodlands" of Eastern Europe—and Luke, seeing the book on my desk, came to me and asked how I could possibly be adding one more brick to the already immense wailing wall that memorialized the Jewish Holocaust, while having written nothing in my life about the Belgian one. The Congo genocide, as he was learning, references the period around 1900 when King Leopold II of Belgium, in pursuit of increased rubber production, enforced a horrific series of cruelties on the Congolese population. A private army was allowed to mutilate resisters at will—hands and limbs were chopped off, routinely. (Go look at the photographs, if you can bear to!) Though many of the dead were killed by disease rather than directly by the Europeans, the diseases were caused by the social devastation of the colonial exploitation, which the region still hasn't recovered from. Guesses at the number killed run all the way up to ten million; certainly, Congolese society was destroyed.

Now, Belgium under King Leopold, in those years, was not, strictly speaking, a liberal democracy—but let us not take false comfort in that fact. It existed well within the concert of Europe, shared a pleasure-seeking civilization and, in Brussels, a Belle Époque capital, as well as supposed progressive values with the other European nations. In many ways its special brutality was simply a way of trying to catch up with already well-established imperialisms.

That's part of the classic leftist critique of liberalism. We point to the peace and prosperity and pluralism of liberal societies and compare them complacently to the cruelties of competing systems—but all we *really* do is export our horrors elsewhere where we don't have to look at them. We export them to what's now called the third or developing world, to Africa or to Asia and Latin America; Americans historically exported them out West, to our own indigenous peoples. (Let us never forget that Hitler modeled his own genocidal invasion of Ukraine and Belorussia and the rest, and what was done to the unwanted "natives" there, on what America had done to the indigenous people of *its* western region—Hitler thought that killing all the Jews and a lot of the Slavs was just "clearing out the Indians" and making the land safe for European settlement, too.)

Liberal prosperity and pluralism are great, sure—all you have to do is discount the racism, sexism, cruelty, and the long centuries of exploitation and continuing despoiling of other people's cultures, environments, and goods. Liberal reform is pious—until it runs up against the limits of what it won't, or can't, reform, which is the governing system of exploitation and oppression. It sends *that* out freely to everyone too weak to resist.

Even as the United States was exporting liberal democracy to Western Europe after the Second World War and supporting it there—while endlessly contrasting it with the tepid totalitarianism of Eastern Europe—in Latin America, at the same time, we were exporting not liberal democracy but brutal military rule. We did this on our behalf and that of the multinational corporations that made their money exploiting Latin Americans. Liberal democracy only operates within an extremely narrow range of classes and colors and countries. I've been praising the parliamentary records and maneuverings of Gladstone and Disraeli, nineteenth-century British statesmen, but they look very different, and a lot less admirable, to the people in Africa and Asia who had to fight against the domination that both British liberals and constitutional conservatives wrought. From an Indian point of view, Gladstone and Disraeli and their predecessors and the massed guns staring down the "mutineers" during the 1857 rebellion in India were all the same person.

That's an *ancient* assault on the very idea of democracy and its publicists, by the way. Fifth-century BCE Athens was a democracy. But its democracy was not only restricted to the predictable groups—men, with no slaves or women involved—it was also practiced at an enormous imperial cost to the non-Athenians. The Athenian League was, like the British Empire, an imperialist project through which the Athenians asserted their democratic glory, while plundering everybody else's goods. I once visited a beautiful little temple on the island of Antiparos, which had been long buried because it had been brutally sacked and burned down by the democracy-loving Athenians, after the people of the larger adjoining island of Paros wouldn't immediately bow down and pay the required tribute to the great democrats coming down with their navy to civilize them. America, the argument goes, is only too true to the Athenian model. The American role in creating and supporting oppressive military governments in Latin America—in Chile and Argentina and Nicaragua and so many other places—makes us their unfortunate inheritors.

The leftist critique of liberalism isn't only or exclusively or even primarily a critique of its role outside the liberal countries. The radical assault is just as much, or even more, on liberalism's failures within its own societies: bourgeois liberalism is not merely incidentally exploitative and inequitable, it is intrinsically and incurably exploitative and inequitable. The worst thing liberalism does is exploit its atrocities downward. "Free societies," as a matter of practical fact, always mean free-market societies—and free markets will never sponsor more than predatory capitalism. Inequalities don't often emerge. They *always* emerge, and their emergence creates greater and greater injustice and despair. The numbers are clear—but the world the numbers make are even clearer to open eyes. New York is filled with sky-high condominium complexes designed only to park the money of the super-rich: the recently built tower at 432 Park Avenue—I call it the oligarch's erection—is the highest and most pillar-like of them. The comedian Chris Rock, rich himself, says, accurately, that if ordinary people knew the way the rich really live, they would riot. (I had recalled that he was talking about the luxuries of private air travel but discovered on checking that he was merely talking about the lesser luxury of first-class flight.) Rock also makes a nice distinction between being rich, which normal people can sometimes achieve, and having wealth, which is still the special province of a tiny inherited class. The freedom of the agora is really just the dictatorship of the drachma: we all depend for our place on how much we have in our pockets and therefore must live our lives in someone else's.

※

Now, the distinction between leftists and liberals, or between radicals and liberals as it's perhaps better put, is one that has a long and extremely complicated history. Though the left-liberal chimera of panicked right-wing propaganda is a fabulous beast, forcing together in one fevered imagination two incompatible animals, the distinctions do change and blur and emerge only over time, as all living distinctions must. Though more radical and more moderate factions—Jacobins and Girondins—existed during the French Revolution, the differences between them were based on very different premises than the ones we know now: the extreme Jacobins under Robespierre, for instance, were *more* insistently religious or deist than those gathered around the otherwise more moderate faction. Some radicals were radicals for free entrepreneurship; some moderates, in the French manner, were more inclined to a centralized state.

Then, in the early nineteenth century, people called liberals were distinct from those called radicals or socialists because liberals were still—as they are to this day, in the French sense of the term—above all aligned with the free market against state control. But this was far from a neat "liberal or conservative" placement in our sense either, since being aligned with the free market meant being *against* the aristocratic oligarchy and its monopolies. This is what made Adam Smith a hero to one whole wing of the French revolutionary movement. Being a liberal didn't mean aligning in consolidation with power but protesting power in the interests of the entrepreneurial middle classes. That's the sense in which the so-called Lunar Society, the circle in the British midlands around Josiah Wedgewood, Erasmus Darwin, and Joseph Wright of Derby, were politically liberal even in their entrepreneurship—making and selling popular plates enabled new kinds of ideas to flourish outside oligarchic control. But nor did being a liberal mean being a democrat in our sense. One could be a liberal, in favor of freedom from aristocratic domination, without being at all in favor of broad enfranchisement of the working classes or having absolute faith in free elections to settle governments.

Nonetheless, by our pivotal decade of the 1860s, those two trends, radical and liberal, were becoming more distinct and the marriage of liberalism with democracy clearer, even though the words used might be different. In Trollope's parliamentary novels, the most beautiful barometer of nineteenth-century British political temperament, the radicals, like Mr. Monk and Mr. Turnbull, are actually what we would now call liberals: opposed to the oligarchic order and to hereditary power and by now in favor of mass enfranchisement, but not social revolutionaries in any sense. Over time, the world has, so to speak, shifted left—one sign of the success of reformism. The people who at the time were thought of as radicals are closer to what we think of as liberals, while Trollope's liberals are closer to what we think of as constitutional conservatives. Certainly, returning to our primal rhino cage, John Stuart Mill, who rightly seems to us now the quintessential liberal philosopher, called himself a socialist in economics and entered Parliament as what was then thought of as a radical. So, democratic-minded radicals and liberty-praising liberals were already beginning to meld into one strain.

But at around that same time, a genuinely distinct radical leftist alternative to liberalism began to rise too. The 1864 meeting in London of the Workingmen's Association—which Karl Marx, whose *Communist Manifesto* was already almost twenty years old, attended—marked, as George Henry Lewes recognized with his quick political intelligence, a decisive and permanent fault line in the political universe. This grouping of leftists—Marx would, like Jefferson, write the program for the organization almost alone—were revolutionary radicals in a way that the liberal tradition Lewes inhabited, descended from Mill, was not and had no intention of becoming. The distinction between liberals, of the Lewes and Eliot and Mill kind, and radicals, of the Marxist order, was coming clearly into view. Though sharing a common sense that much was wrong and something had to be done about it, they were opposed to each other, as they are to this day, about almost every significant question of *what* was wrong, what to do about it, and how best to get it done.

Basically, radicals ever since have accepted Marx's analysis of bourgeois society, while liberals have rejected it. The radical critique of liberalism has asserted, from that time to this, that liberal reform will always be inadequate to the problems of modern capitalist society—all liberalism can do is put Band-Aids on plague sores. The right accompanying adjective for liberalism is not *humane*, as in liberal humanism, but *bourgeois*—and bourgeois liberalism is simply capitalist exploitation in a Sunday park.

The left-wing assault, though focused on the impotence of reform, is sometimes also focused on the liberal idea of *reason*—but that's because radicals have, from that time to this, believed that liberal reason isn't reasonable enough and is merely a cover-up of power relations that liberals don't want to examine. Liberal reasoning is like doing arithmetic without looking at the results. When we actually work out the liberal addition, all the solutions are in the minus column. If mass impoverishment is no longer as acute within the capitalist countries, that is because much of it has been exported to the developing world. I've met people who generously contribute to worthy causes but spend their business lives finding ever-cheaper places in the developing countries to manufacture clothing. When China got too expensive, the T-shirts were made by poorer paid workers in Vietnam, and when even Vietnam turned too expensive, Haiti became the factory. Liberalism, in this view, doesn't just export its atrocities; it exports its exploitations and then brings back the profits to support the supposedly liberal arts.

Marx remains the most formidable critic of liberalism because he stripped away the allure of the language of universality and reason to show the raw power relationships that liberalism enforces. The classic Marxist account shows liberalism simply as the ideology of the bourgeoisie: the people who owned property and had capital to invest, some working as direct exploiters or owners, others working as professionals attending on the owners. In the same way that the Great Chain of Being had been the convenient ideology of the feudal age, liberalism was the convenient ideology of the capitalist one. Medieval priests told the peasants that God had put a fixed hierarchy in place, one that began with God at the top followed by angels and demons and then the church and king and lords, with commoners dangling precariously just above the wild and domesticated animals. Modern clerics, that is to say, liberal philosophers and professors, put another "normal" order in place to cloak the oppressive power relationships of capitalism. They told the proletariat a similar fiction, but instead of God, history and human nature ordered the chain. In this chain, one's place was not ordained but supposedly earned. The people on top had got there by merit; the ones below would have to try harder.

The "reforms" of which liberals never tire of self-praising are simply a series of grudging and partial concessions to popular pressure—ways of opening a steam valve to relieve those pressures and avoid blowing up the ship. Meanwhile letting a few lucky poor folks shimmy part way up the liberal chain of being to keep the others thinking they can, too. The parliamentary proceduralism, of which liberals boast, is still another way of *preventing* change from happening—designed for the most part to corrupt and co-opt potential resistance. Liberals self-praise freedom of speech—but since all their speech is implanted within a capitalist order in which money is the only real medium of exchange, that claim of freedom for all isn't merely partial but deliberately fraudulent. What liberals call free speech or a free press is invariably *paid* speech—and William Randolph Hearst or, these days, Rupert Murdoch can pay for a lot more of it than a sweatshop worker can. The ground of liberalism in open debate sounds cozy until you price it; the coffeehouse is closed to anyone who can't pay for the pastry.

Even at those moments when actual change seems about to take place—as with the emancipation of African Americans or the partial enfranchisement of the British working classes in the same era—the system shuts the lid down tight right after. Jim Crow comes right after Reconstruction; colonial wars drew off the newly empowered working classes to die in foreign fields.

⚜

I wouldn't want to suggest that everyone who criticizes liberalism from the left is a Marxist or derives his or her ideas from his. Some of the most intriguing and convincing of the individual leftists who hate liberalism tend to come from the very different anarchist tradition. Descended from such Russian thinkers as Peter Kropotkin and Mikhail Bakunin, they combine in arresting ways—though I suppose *arresting* isn't the word to use for anarchists—a genuine libertarian impulse, almost too extravagant even for a liberal to accept, along with an authentic indignation at poverty and misery, almost too acute for a liberal to endure. The anarchist tradition is a humanist one, too, though violently antiliberal and often, to a liberal, obsessed with the strange idea of saving humanity by bombing it into freedom.

With no one did the spirit of rebellious humanity burn brighter than the anarchist, activist philosopher, and memoirist—and, truth be told, assassin's accomplice—of the early part of the twentieth century, Emma Goldman. A lovable terrorist seems like a contradiction in terms, but Goldman was certainly lovable, and if she did not directly engage in terrorism, she was certainly not remote from acts that can only be called so. She tells her story in two volumes of autobiography, still completely worth re-reading.

It is hard for a liberal to come away from them not loving her courage and sheer fortitude and entrancing humanity. The furthest thing in the world from a cold fish ideologue, her memoir is filled with accounts of her love affairs and her theatrical passions. She admired and understood Eugene O'Neill before almost anyone else did, and in the midst of her ostracism by the left in Britain in the 1920s after her disillusioning stay in the Soviet Union, she was still sufficiently aesthetic to insist on giving a lecture series not on socialism or Bolshevism but on the making of the American Little Theatre Movement, a once very important groundswell dedicated to popular, participatory drama. Her writings breathe her natural solidarity with other women and are rife, too, with recollected pleasures, in a way that those of almost any other radical writer of the time, the great Max Eastman excepted, are not. She writes delightedly of racing the high tide across the dunes of Provincetown toward safety and the sands. She has a spontaneous humor about all the absurdities of the radical life, including how one red boyfriend, Ben, suddenly turned and, sentimentally, stubbornly, insisted on having a child, with her playing a conventional mother's role. Not only that, but this family drama was set against a history of persecution that even those of us who recall the absurdities of the FBI's war against the civil rights movement in the sixties can't quite credit.

Arriving in America in 1885 from Russia, already radicalized by her experience of oppression both as a woman and

Jew, she soon after found herself at the center of a rich and literary circle in the cafés of New York's Lower East Side. (How essential cafés are not just for liberal but for radical ground! Social capital was and remains essential to anti-capitalism.) She was one of those people with such a natural gift for speaking to the masses that she was forced into a leadership role almost before she could speak enough English to reach the actual masses outside her own neighborhood. Reading her now, one is stunned not only at her engagement with the struggle for workers' rights—at a time when unionizing was often a crime and the bosses had no compunction about sending mobs of vigilantes and paid thugs out to beat and even kill strikers—but even more by her openness to new realms of sexual liberation. At one point, she went to work as a midwife, and she writes piteously about the demands of working-class women for abortion—women with five or six children already and barely able to feed them. Even Goldman couldn't risk providing abortions herself, at the time of the Comstock Laws, when contraception itself was illegal and organized religion did all it could to keep it from becoming even remotely acceptable. (Anyone who thinks of abortion as a rich woman's privilege should read Goldman and be reminded of the huge human cost of having children without contraception.)

But then one of the things that makes her so moving as a person is the story of her own enthusiastic sexual awakening. She writes about her lovers (many hapless) with enormous humanity and candor. She recognized the deep tension, bound to be true in the life of any activist, between the devotion to a cause, an ideal, and the price you pay for it in your personal life—and that price is becoming dehumanized, ever less aware of the real wellsprings of pleasure in human life that you are ostensibly fighting to spread and share. Where the other socialist movements of the time tended to be highly patriarchal, her anarchism was uniquely sensitive to women's issues. She even writes, with an audacity still startling today, about her encounter with a young and closeted lesbian and how she encouraged her to express herself erotically. Later generations of feminists reproduced T-shirts with a motto supposedly taken from Emma Goldman: "If I Can't Dance, I Don't Want to Be Part of Your Revolution." The words are probably not precisely hers, but that's her spirit; she dances through her autobiography instead of narrating it.

Her life included several moments of extraordinary moral courage—and others of extraordinary moral ambiguity. In 1892, she helped her lover, the anarchist philosopher and activist Alexander Berkman (always affectionately called Sasha in her memoirs), to buy a gun to shoot Henry Clay Frick in Pittsburgh. (Frick, a tycoon as much as an art collector, had encouraged the mass killing of striking steel workers at Homestead, far from his Fifth Avenue mansion.) It was, on its own terms, a delicately moral "anarchism of the deed": Berkman insisted on being in the presence of Frick alone, without potential collateral targets, even servants. But it *was* an act of terrorism, an assassination of an unarmed businessman. Frick, shot, didn't die. (Goldman believed forever after, realistically, that Berkman failed because they didn't have the cash to buy a better brand of pistol.) Berkman, somewhat miraculously, went to prison for just over a decade—in brutal conditions, yes, but these days he'd spend the rest of his life in a single room in a supermax prison with no hope for parole. When he got out, he was able to write a classic of anarchist political literature, *The ABC of Communist Anarchism*—a strange book, as much a libertarian as an anarchist manifesto.

And, make no mistake, Emma Goldman was no friend to American liberals or liberalism, as she experienced them. Imprisoned in 1917 for helping poor men resist the draft for what she saw, not without reason, as a crazy imperialist war, on her release in 1919 she and Berkman were deported, through the shameful Immigration Act and particularly at the behest of a young and already vicious J. Edgar Hoover. The decision was met with minimal liberal protest. Liberal Americans, she decided, were the weakest and the most easily panicked and stampeded people in the world. The Great War was a moment not unlike the aftermath of 9/11: fear easily got the better of liberal principle, so quickly and completely that it was easy to see the principles of liberalism as no more than shiny gift-wrap, all torn off in a moment. Reading her memoirs one shudders to think if any liberal of her time, or of this one, could have recovered from imprisonment, banishment, deportation, hunger, and abandonment and remained hopeful, energetic, and alert enough to the absurdities of existence to keep writing and bearing witness.

Exiled to the newly Bolshevik Russia, she expected, if not utopia, then at least a step toward it. But, and this was one of her acts of greatest moral courage, she immediately recognized—long before it was fashionable, not to say acceptable—that the new-made world in Russia was a nightmare, not merely misguided in its excesses but evil from the start. Bakunin had been right in 1867 when he predicted that "liberty without socialism is injustice; socialism without liberty is slavery and brutality." Lenin, whom Emma met, was obviously a brutal tyrant and the Communist system under him a betrayal of the workers, with bloodlust as its first principle. She said this loudly and often and presciently and courageously. Half a century later, most of her friends on the left were still reluctant even to whisper the same truths.

As always happens to brave people who speak first, she got no credit for it from her enemies and only the increased hatred of her soon-to-be ex-friends. Still known only as Red Emma, despite having defied the reds, she had to flee, first to Germany, then London, and eventually to Canada, where she spoke often in Winnipeg and Montreal and died, aged seventy, in Toronto. Throughout her life, she never compromised either the purity of her anarchist and sensualist and libertarian principles in the face of left-wing totalitarianism—she polemicized during the Civil War in Spain, but only on the (doomed) Anarchist side—or in the face of what she saw as pervasive liberal weakness. Even more astonishing, she never sold out her pleasures to those principles. Hating Frick didn't mean you had to hate the Frick Collection; it just meant you wanted Fragonard's *The Progress of Love* to be available to poor people as well as rich people, not just as a picture series but as an ideal. She was a democratic sensualist by instinct, an anarchist liberty lover by creed, and her life and thought is a permanent reproach to what she saw as the sheer *timidity* of liberalism, its inability to reach up high for a yet unimagined ideal.

These days, Goldman's spirit of sensual abandon combined with hard-core anarchism—a love sonnet in one hand, a stick of dynamite in the other—is less present in leftist circles. But the anarchist insistence that the idea of revolution against the bourgeois order has no meaning if it proceeds from mere economic rearrangements—that it had instead to take aim at the very core of our entire existence, become part of our sex lives and the way we dance even more than the mere way we vote or work—has had an inescapable after life. Though more post-Marxist than truly anarchist in spirit, most left-wing critiques of liberalism now do turn more often on its cultural power and its cultural illusions than on the narrower, classically Marxist terms of how the workers get organized and who pays them when they do.

In the original Marxist analysis, the bourgeoisie ruled the oppressed through direct means of coercion: if you struck, they would call in the strikebreakers or the police or even the army to shoot you. But over time, massacres of the workers became less frequent even as capitalism, in leftist eyes at least, was freed more and more from the shackles of the state. For us self-satisfied liberals, the reduction in obvious class violence meant the world was actually getting more prosperous and class relations less fixed and oppressive. For the radical-left critics of liberalism, by contrast, the oppression had only become more pervasive and insidious. Nowadays, the massacres of the working classes pass more quietly, through obesity and opioid addiction and other cultural instruments, rather than through direct power. They don't have to send the army to coerce you because capitalist culture has coerced you already. The whole end of liberal culture and self-advertisement—including, of course, books like this one—is not only, as in the classic analysis, to make a brutal power relationship look normal. It is to make that same brutality look *natural*, just the way things are. The entirety of liberal culture works—not conspiratorially, at the direction of a few mustache-twirling puppet masters, but simply in the way that all cultures work, by the systematic infection of minds—to infest value, literature, and language itself so that oppression looks like life.

The triumphs of this kind of post-Marxism have meant that the focus of radical complaints has shifted: from being above all economic they have become above all *cultural*, with the economic issues trailing behind. This may be in part a selection effect: while the suffering goes on on the factory floor, or in the absence of any factory floor to suffer on, the talking goes on in college classrooms. I don't doubt that, among the admirable remaining veterans engaged in union organization and economic opportunity, fundamental economic questions still matter. We may even be on the brink of a revival of classical labor-socialist politics, if the rise of the Democratic Socialists of America—or, at least, their burst into the public consciousness—is any indication.

Certainly, a new swear word has emerged. *Neoliberalism* may be the single most commonly used term in left polemics right now—though, a liberal might think, one with the vaguest specific referent in all of political language. (*Fascist*, to be fair, has something of the same range, being used to condemn actual fascists and gym teachers.) Neoliberal is meant to label the spread of absolutist free-market doctrines, in the wake of the end of the Cold War, and the surrender, presumably shared by self-described progressive liberals as much as by unapologetic libertarians, to the doctrine that all social life should be seconded to the market. It's what is supposed to have produced our current planetary disturbance and our planetary populist protest.

But for most of the past thirty years, for good or ill, questions about labor and the shop floor have become less central to radical criticism of liberalism, and questions of gender, race, language, and sexual orientation ever more so. This reflects the basic American situation in which the right wing wants cultural victories and gets nothing but political ones; while the left wing wants political victories and gets only cultural ones. It is possible to see this as a massive distraction for progressive causes, in which the left manages to get sombreros banned from college parties while every federal court in the country is assigned a far-right-wing activist judge. Or (as the right often does) as a fiendishly perverse victory. If you control the schools, you control the school kids; the Jesuits operated on this truth for centuries. Even the working classes that used to be "heroized" in leftist thought are now, as grad students would say, "problematized," exactly because they tend to be the source of so much of the bigotry and persecution that women, gays, and blacks feel.

Not surprisingly, the white Europeans' pet achievement, the so-called Enlightenment of the eighteenth century, has become the original villain of the story. The moment when liberalism is conventionally imagined to be born is actually when its pretensions died. In the left's account of history, the Enlightenment had as its end not the liberation of men and women from superstition and tradition but the reordering of the world in the interests of European power. The Enlightenment transformed racism from bigoted folklore into pseudoscientific laws and rooted the oppression of women not just in custom but in the pseudoscience of medicine. Sporadic cruelty became systematic punishment, the masked executioner traded places with the prison warden and solitary confinement, all in the name of "objective" science. Giovanni Piranesi with his prisons and dungeons is a truer artist of the Enlightenment than David Hume with his skepticism and sympathy.

⚜

But the left tradition isn't only devoted to analyzing the insidious cultural meanings of phallocentric narratives and pumpkin spice lattés. In recent years a new kind of activist left has emerged into mainstream culture and advanced a lucid theoretical analysis of class and race. This new politics paints a familiar, broad picture of oppression through cultural framing and control, but it's inflected by the new concept of "intersectionality" and tied in complicated ways to what we often call identity politics.

Intersectionality is a scare word on the right, a pious and little understood word among the more cautious left. But when you read the central theorists of intersectionality—bell hooks (Gloria Jean Watkins) or Kimberle Crenshaw, for example—you find that it's an impressively ambitious effort to offer a unified field theory of cultural and economic oppression. The concerns of various groups—the oppression of women, gays, and black people, the marginalization of other sexual minorities—may seem like separate issues. Indeed, many dedicated liberal activists have long treated them as such, seeking to free blacks first, women second, and Latinos later on. But they *intersect* in significant ways to create repeated local nodes of oppression and identity. They stack in many specific shapes. Crucially, you see that these differences are *essential*—difference is who we are, and defining your difference is what liberalism doesn't want you to do. Instead of dismissing difference in the solvent of liberal universalism, the intersectional theorist argues that people should unashamedly emphasize it—speak out as black women or gay Hispanic men, not be silenced or forced to speak in a voice not their own. And when a white dude speaks up, perhaps with a complaint, everyone must become aware that *he* is speaking not as some disinterested observer but as a straight, cis-gendered white man with the interests, prejudices, and history of his kind.

The Anita Hill hearings of 1991 are a good indice—and perhaps originally an igniting incident—of intersectionalist thinking. Anita Hill spoke up about her long history of sexual harassment at the hands of Clarence Thomas, of his banter designed to humiliate and disquiet her. Despite the obvious truthfulness of her testimony—and, a fact forgotten now, its immediate support in testimony from other women—she was both doubted and then ignored as Thomas called on the old specter of lynching ("it is a high-tech lynching") to justify himself. Neither the understanding of racial oppression, focused on black men, nor that of women's liberation, focused on middle-class white women, could provide a cultural place for a black woman, or blackwoman, as some would prefer, to be heard. The intersection of her oppression as both black and a woman made her invisible on the usual grid. We not only ought to have heard her as Anita Hill but as a black woman with a history of enforced silencing shared with countless others. Treating her as an individual witness alone cheated her voice of its true resonance. Overlapping identities enlist overlapping systems of subordination, in ways that can't be caught by simple addition: someone can be black and lesbian and working class, but one can't just add one oppression onto another. These different oppressions interact in specific ways. Midcentury sexism kept middle-class white women home and sent working-class black women to work for them. Their interests and experiences are different.

There are essentially two strong forces in intersectionality's unified field theory of oppression. One is the othering by which the dominant culture makes marginalized groups alien and prevents them not just from being heard but from speaking at all in their own voices—the force by which black men and boys are reduced from human beings to frightening, faceless superpredators who can only be policed and controlled. The other force is the positive engine of difference, by which the oppressed can assert their own commonalities and by which those marginalized find their own voices, unashamedly at the intersection of their own identities, not some other.

The assertion of difference is a way of countering the insidious coercions of mainstream liberal culture. The "color-blind" universe of "neutral" liberalism is actually an attempt to erase cultural identity and history, as the centuries-old split between black nationalists and black integrationists demonstrates. Liberals piously insist on color-blind equality of opportunity, when they are just removing the reality of history and race. *Plessy v. Ferguson*, the notorious "separate but equal" Supreme Court decision, though officially outdated, reflects this distortion, and this distortion still lives. Both black and white are treated as equivalent constructions, when they clearly have wildly different histories and uses—and the labels create wildly different effects on those so labeled. Though legally outmoded, the concept remains intact in the permanent monument of white people's disingenuousness. Equal lingers on as a concept even if separate is officially discarded. If blacks and whites are essentially equal, why would either need anything more than balanced equality of opportunity? Though begun in the investigation of race relations, the intersectional theorist's attempt to reject othering while insisting on difference has proven powerful for other groups as well. The #MeToo movement is unimaginable without this intellectual groundwork. Women who have been silenced—sometimes literally—suddenly can "sing the silence" of their inner lives.

That's the way in which intersectionality is sometimes seen as the academic version or foundation—or perhaps, depending on how you date its evolution, the side effect—of what are now called identity politics. Different groups, liberals are said to have long insisted, should be forged together by practical politics into a single umbrella unit and asked to look past their specificities. By contrast, intersectional politics say that we should look at our specificities and unashamedly recognize and assert them in our politics. The emphatic assertion of difference (I am and speak as a gay Hispanic man, I am and speak as an Asian lesbian woman), with its refusal to accept the idea that what we actually are is in some way lesser or other, is the first premise of liberation. It is also from this kind of analysis that the pervasive critique of white privilege arises. White people in America are so entrenched in their own unearned entitlements that they mistake them for a natural state. They've been living in their own intersection so long they can't even see the traffic.

⇛

The liberal response to left-wing radicalism has, historically, always been rhetorically weak—even though, historically, it has also been demonstrably correct. I doubt that I can fully remedy that. The rhetorical weakness is apparent on any college campus today. Who would not rather be fiercely radical than circumspectly liberal? Who would not rather inherit some of the passion of the romantic movement and its rebellions rather than settle for all those parenthetical qualifications and rhinoceros-like snortings? It is much easier to convert smart people to a view of the necessities of massive social renewal than to the exigencies of small-step social reform. Since the French Revolution the entirety of Western politics has been practiced on a moral slope canted left. Indeed, people in France used to have a saying: "Better to be wrong with Sartre than right with Aron." (That I now probably have to explain that Raymond Aron was a great conservative-liberal thinker in France, right about far more things in the world, from Stalinism to the Resistance, than Sartre ever was, is in itself a sign of the inequality of treatment.) This is one of the things that infuriates constitutional conservatives about liberals when they debate and argue with one another: liberals always assume, and are usually granted, the moral high ground even if it is made up of the refuse of old pieties and half-baked rectitude.

Well, if it's any comfort, liberals feel the same way about leftists: they convert kids readily, while the objections we liberals can offer always feel as feeble as a dad telling a teenage girl that she should be very careful riding in cars with other teens who drink. You sound like a schmuck compared to the cool boy who drives seat-belt-less with artfully tossed Hunter Thompson paperbacks on the backseat.

But that dad is simply, invariably *right*—driving drunk is an insane practice, and the liberal reproach to leftism is right, too, on more or less the same basis: driving intoxicated on the rhetoric of revolutionary change is crazy, especially in light of all the road fatalities already recorded. The romantic utopian visions, put in place, always fail and usually end in a horrific car crash.

There is a tragic rule of twenty-first-century life, a rule of double amnesia: the right tends to act as though the nineteenth century never happened, while the left tends to act as though the twentieth century never took place. The right acts as if the socialist responses to capitalism—economic planning, the welfare state, even Keynesian economics—were the result of crazy abstract ideas of statism imposed on a pliant population by power-mad intellectuals, not, as they actually were, initial responses to mass immiseration and the daily show of extreme poverty and the relentless anxiety that industrial capitalism had produced. The left treats the obvious and inarguable lessons of the twentieth century about radical revolutions—lessons about the failure of revolution in the absence of free speech and open debate, of parliamentary procedures and small-scale experiments in change—as though they had never been learned and learned in the hardest of hard ways. On the left, the product is not just post-Marxism but what I call ghost-Marxism, an eagerness to use the old vocabulary of revolution with zero recognition of the history of what happens when the solutions are actually attempted. It is the *language* of revolution completely divorced from the evidence of experience.

The liberal response to left-wing views, old and new, is, first, that economic injustice is self-evidently amendable within the liberal order, if we have the will to do it. Second, that while the new radical assault on liberalism suggests a passionate politics, it still doesn't propose a *practical* politics—one that seems likely to win elections rather than impress sophomores at Sarah Lawrence. (That is said without disdain; I have subsidized a sophomore at Sarah Lawrence.) And finally—in a way that may seem more tediously abstract but actually is a day-to-day effect on our thinking—that the new radical critiques all depend on forms of determinism and essentialism that have in the past always rightly been seen as reactionary and will still prove false friends to progressive causes.

To begin with, economic issues peculiar to capitalism have to be separated from those pervasive in modernity. When, for instance, contemporary leftists treat the environmental disasters that frighten us all as capitalism's war against the planet—or, worse, of neoliberalism against the planet—they are engaged in a campaign that is, from a historical point of view, absurd. Environmental disasters are the right thing to be worried about, but it is the drive for growth, not capitalism in particular, that makes them happen. The degree and level of environmental disaster caused by the command economics of Eastern Europe were far greater than even the worst known in Western Europe and was made still worse by a state-controlled media that could not even wave a feeble flag of dissent. What happened to Lake Baikal under the Soviets never happened to an American Great Lake. The villain in our environmental disasters may well be the common fault of modernity and of industrialization. But to understand pollution as a problem owed to capitalism is to understand nothing. This is ghost Marxism: a will to repeat the same old curses and haunt the same old houses without having the confidence to go outside and see the world as it really is.

This inability to see things as they exist is only intensified by those intimidating-sounding habits of essentialism and determinism. Determinism is the belief, encountered already, that an insidious hegemonic network of enforced linguistic habits and instilled prejudices in our culture blind us from seeing the true nature of power relationships—not just slant us or partly shape our responses but really *blind* us, prevent us from seeing how the oppressed get oppressed. We can't see past the categories of our traditions or hear past the stereotypes of our language.

Now, obviously, these traps must be among the weakest ever devised by man since they can apparently be dispelled by a semester in a decent progressive high school. The idea, for instance, that language creates a trap for our cognition or puts a straitjacket on it, forcing us into one worldview or another, is one of the oldest and most frequently (if futilely) dispelled of modern ideas.

The argument over pronouns is a good example of the tendency on the left to turn a question of courtesy into a question of cognition. This argument runs that using masculine pronouns in preference to feminine ones for collective nouns, as has been the rule in English for centuries, is inherently sexist and helps shape our minds in a patriarchal direction. We should use *her* and *hers* in preference to *him* and *his* and allow people to invent their own pronouns to opt out of any gender-based hierarchy—using, say, *they* and *them.*

As a matter of courtesy, we should, indeed, always respect other people's pronouns as we should respect their proper nouns. What someone wishes to be called is what they ought to be called. As a matter of cognitive fact, however, we should not think that *any* words, including pronouns, can compel thoughts we don't want to have. The system of genders in French, for instance—where every object in the world is either masculine or feminine—does not in any discernible way alter the realities, or challenges, of feminism in that country or language. Simone de Beauvoir wrote in the same gendered French as her backward contemporaries.

A whole industry may exist to coerce and conceal, but an equally large social practice also exists to reveal the absurdities of it: we call it conversation and, particularly, comedy. It's hard not to know what's going on. We may not be able to change it, but we know it. Blindness to our circumstances is not really a problem. (Noam Chomsky, a family hero, insists that our consent is manipulated and our free speech controlled, but no one on earth has had less trouble being fully and comprehensively heard than Noam Chomsky. What he is not is universally *agreed* with—a very different thing.)

But aren't working-class people still effectively coerced to misperceive their own interests by the fog that capitalism places over their eyes, all those distractions, both of entertainments and of enforced resentments? Certainly, the deepest, most untouchable—or incurable—of all twentieth-century left beliefs are that the working class of any nation is intrinsically progressive and votes for nationalist right-wing leaders, whose interests obviously align with the very wealthy, out of deliberately planted confusion and "false consciousness." No matter how many times this happens, or in how many places, and how resistant to persuasion the prejudices of the working class turn out to be, it is still the firm conviction of those on the left that the people would be with us if they could only see their own interests clearly.

I don't mean to underestimate the power that, for instance, the Murdoch media empire possesses or the asymmetry between how much the right and left can pay for public speech. All of this is real. But the pattern of working-class people who ought to be progressive and aren't is, historically, far too widespread across too many different countries and eras to be simply explicable in this way. We say that working people are *distracted* by those wealthy propagandists by social issues. But one might just as well say that their attention is being *drawn* to the social issues—to the truth that if they align with progressives who might give them Medicare for all, they will also be giving them power to legalize gay marriage and transgender bathrooms and other deeply antitraditional choices. We may not share these choices, but we shouldn't condescend to them. It's the same thing in reverse that conservative Jews say about liberal Jews: How can they not see their own interests and instead "vote

like Puerto Ricans"? That liberal Jews are willing to forgo
their immediate interests in, say, lower taxes for the larger
good of protecting the civil liberties that they believe have
been essential for Jewish survival is no more nor less rational than that of the Christian believer who sacrifices medical insurance to ward off gay wedding cakes. Ours not to
reason the priorities, our own priorities being, in their own
way, equally "unreasonable," that is, reflective of our values,
not our interests. Coerced consciousness is much less powerful in the real world than conscious conviction. We have
to work to change the convictions, and then the supposedly
superintending "consciousness" will change, too.

⋘⃰⋙

It seems odd, I know, to say that an epistemological error
is behind an electoral failure—but sometimes mistakes in
thinking really can lead to mistakes in tactics, and the embrace of what's called essentialism by progressive-minded
people is an instance of this kind. Essentialism is the idea,
descending from Plato and coursing through the blood-
stream of Western thought, that we arrive at reliable knowledge only by figuring out the *true nature* of something,
which is fixed, eternal, and durable. The essence of a thing
is that thing. Essentialism makes us ask what-is questions:
What is time? What is space? What is human nature? Or
more locally: What is a woman? What is black? What is the
essence of the Jew?

Against this view are the nominalists, triumphant in the
natural sciences, who tell us that these what-is questions
lead nowhere. A scientific theory of gravity does not ask,

what is gravity? Rather, it tries to explain through a testable theory exactly why and how and by what specific rules apples fall from trees—and then appends the name of gravity as a shorthand label to the result. Darwin didn't ask, what is a duck? He studied the way that variation in individuals produce common kinds and knew that we then append the name of duck as a postscript to our observations. Gravity doesn't have an essence; not even ducks have an essence.

A fair criticism of the contemporary left is that it is as essentialist as it needs to be at some moments—and then as wildly antiessentialist as possible at immediately adjacent ones. Studying the left-wing attack on liberalism, we find a map of what might be called opportunistic essentialism. Kids are taught in progressive schools that all gender is fluid and constructed—except for that of transgender kids, which is an absolute and essential feature, locked in early, never to be questioned. All racial groups are constructions, too— except for that of whiteness, which can be rightly treated as an undifferentiated actual thing, an essence shared by its holders that warps their views and disables their thinking. This belief is held, even though the range and late arrival of participants in whiteness are the best possible demonstration that no racial essence ever exists. We see this ambiguity in the overpublicized contested cases—someone claims to be Jewish who has a Jewish father or mother; someone claims to be black who, well, wants to be. We can insist, with the rabbis, that there's a blood definition of Jewish; or we can insist, with the humanists, that there isn't. But we can't insist on both at the same time.

This is far from an abstract or academic argument. It has everything to do with how we think and talk about freedom and authority in our daily conversation. Essentialism tells us always to ask for the authority behind an idea or to demand the true origin of a person. What is she *really*? it makes us ask. Who said it? Where does it (or her) come from? When the questions we should be asking are: What relation does what's being said have to what actually happens? Or, more simply: Is that true?

The idea that one should trace the source of an argument backward, to its origins, rather than play it forward to the evidence for its claims is the root doctrine of reaction. I have tried in these pages to be skeptical about tying liberalism and science too tightly together. Liberalism preceded modern science, and humanism preceded both—and liberalism does not demand in any way an exclusive commitment to materialism: it is perfectly possible to be a liberal Catholic or a liberal agnostic or a liberal rabbi.

But antiessentialism is exactly the place where the scientific turn of mind and the liberal turn of mind really do meet in a common antiauthoritarianism. *All* that the empirical sciences have given us rests on the radically new belief that an idea is best evaluated by never asking who thought it up and what authority they had to think it but by asking what facts support it and what facts might prove it false.

Some great scientists have been exceptionally admirable people, like Charles Darwin and Einstein; some exceptionally strange people, like Isaac Newton; some exceptionally unpleasant people, like Werner Heisenberg. Some rich, some poor, some racist, some not. But we can say, categorically, that the background and conduct, the class or race, of the man or woman who thought up a scientific theory has nothing whatever to do with the truth or value of that theory as science. The intersection of formative ideas in the biography of a scientist may be an intriguing subject—Darwin's abolitionism certainly had something to do with his evolutionism—but the scientist's identity never marks a theory true or false.

In the past, it was typical of totalitarian movements, and particularly extreme reactionary right-wing ones, to insist that we can *only* evaluate a claim if we first know who is making it and where it comes from. This has produced such notions as the Nazi concept of Jewish physics. Einstein, being a Jew, couldn't be right about the universe; the theory of relativity could be condemned in advance by knowing the essential racial nature of its maker. Those who attacked Frederick Douglass in the pre–Civil War period all insisted that he must be lying about his history as a slave *because* he was black. Modern art is bad because it is the expression of Jews; jazz is bad because it is the music of "Negroes."

Insisting on the origins of an idea as the *test* of an idea's value is a quintessentially reactionary notion—in many ways, it is *the* quintessential reactionary notion. I spoke warmly of G. K. Chesterton in the last chapter, but he was also the most influential anti-Semite in the England of his age, and the core of his anti-Semitism was the belief that Jews are aliens who refuse to be called aliens. This meant that even when they said the right things they were wrong because they were the wrong people to say it; they were impersonators of virtue or of Englishness, who debased the authentic by their touch. This was Chesterton's constant cry about the Jews. If they would just concede their distinct nature, their "Jewishness," we wouldn't have to ostracize them. If they would, for instance, wear distinct clothing, then we would be content to allow them to speak. (Yes, he really proposed that.) An obsession with difference has a way of producing otherness with extraordinary speed and venom.

Enlisting in opportunistic essentialism is a kind of poison that you think you're taking in small quantities for homeopathic purposes, and then you find out it's spread throughout your body. One need only look, for instance, at the class category of the bourgeoisie to see the essentialist fallacy at insidious work. The term was used and is used still to summon up, dismissively, a category and a set of narrow, philistine, material-minded, self-interested pursuers of personal and familial entitlement at the cost of public virtues. Popularized in France—it's a French word, of course—it is still used, sneeringly, to this day. There are bourgeois amenities and bourgeois worldviews and bourgeois Bohemians. There's no quicker formula for dismissing liberal views than to reduce them to bourgeois interests.

But when we try to examine bourgeois for its actual content, it disappears in a cloud of contradictory specifics and invisible individuals. It's an essentialized class with no referent. As the historian Sarah Maza has shown, brilliantly, "it functioned as a critical counter-norm, an imagined and threatening embodiment of materialism, self-interest, commercialism, and mass culture." No one *ever* self-identified as a bourgeois. It was an invention designed to create a convenient counterobject, even a hate object.

Essentializing anything in order to contain or dismiss it is always a false friend to reform. For essentialism *is* extremism, extremism in its denial of plurality, possibility, ambiguity, double usage, multiple identities. The power of nominalism lies in saying this thing can be any number of things; we'll call it when we choose. Giving up essentialism isn't an academic move; it's a way of countering the fanaticism of the single cause. A left critique that employs it, however opportunistically, will soon find itself stranded on the extreme end of public argument. Intersectionalism in a sense does not go far enough. There are countless nodes on the network of social categories. We call each one a person.

So, liberals ask leftists to be extremely suspicious of a too-greedy or opportunistic essentialism that may help dismiss critics today but that undermines the larger project of human emancipation, a project that depends, first and last, on being able to see past categories and types toward actual people and their predicaments. Antiessentialism is the universal solvent of illiberal thought.

With all this in mind we can perhaps return to the vexed question of privilege. Now it is a bit of a tell when all the people arguing against the concept of white privilege are white. Black women, Latino trans-sexuals, and, of course, lots of white people, too, tend to assent emphatically to this idea, while white men are pretty much left alone to dispute it. When white men alone insist that they do not have privileges, then they do.

But privilege is a less interesting name for a more interesting thing, and that is *good fortune*. Good fortune is often given, and it is often earned. Every society known to human history has varying degrees of it. Indeed, every society that we can possibly imagine would have *some* people with better luck than others, if only because of the accidents of sickness and health. (Even hunter-gatherer societies are very far from perfectly egalitarian.) Those who have it are likely to emphasize the parts that were earned by labor, while those who don't have it see the bits that were given at birth. But the ethical choice that good fortune brings remains the same, whether earned or given. Those with good fortune can try to share it, or those with good fortune can decide to hoard it. Between the hoarders and the sharers is a huge historical gap, which defines what liberalism is. It's the space where liberalism begins.

What is meant by white privilege is not so much a historical description of the way in which discrimination has happened but a description of the way in which life proceeds *now*. A black teenager will expect to be treated with unearned mistrust from shopkeepers, taxi drivers, Starbucks baristas, and, worst of all, the police in a way that a white—Jewish or Irish or even Asian—teenager won't.

But, the liberal would argue, is this really a description of white privilege? Isn't it actually a description of white bigotry? (Often tragically extended to other subgroups who come to share the bigotries.) Privilege, after all, ought to be the default condition of *everyone* living as a citizen in a liberal democracy—that is, without any previous assumption about one's own history or predilections. The aim of social reform ought to be to draw more and more people into the privileged category, a point implicitly conceded by the very act of its critics having to pile more and more privileges into that box. Whereas in living memory inherited privilege was the special space of the WASP hierarchy, it now supposedly extends to Jews and even Asians. What are described as privileges are not unearned rights appropriated by a few but fundamental rights that should not be deprived to anyone. This is, yes, liberal universalism, but the reason that liberals are universalists is not because they think that everyone is always one thing but rather that, knowing that everyone *is* many things at once, they want everyone to act with maximum fairness all the time. You can embrace difference and reject discrimination—rejecting discrimination is exactly the reason to embrace difference.

The existence of privilege produces an understandable frustration with its self-replicating power. Privilege really does inhere in inherited money. That's what the Victorian radicals were reacting against. But it does not inhere remotely in the same way in education, which is exactly the means that have given the left the possibility to see past privilege to power. To a first approximation, *all* the radical doctrines that have changed the world have been written from a position of privilege: Kropotkin, the greatest anarchist, was born a prince, the grandson of a Cossack general, with more than a thousand serfs. Marx was an upper-middle-class man with the usual patriarchal prejudices of the kind. My beloved Emma Goldman was underprivileged but hypereducated; education was her lever to equality. All these accomplishments seem self-evidently independent of their origins, just as Darwin was an average husband who shared some of the values of his time and class and completely subverted others. Real life proceeds in tensions and contradictions, not in neatly ordered categories of certainties. Probing exactly for how these contradictions intersect— so that someone can be both a Victorian head of family and the author of ideas that subverted the whole idea of a natural hierarchy—is where real social observation begins. It's what George Eliot watched. It's how emergence happens.

The honest liberal hastens to add that what's now called identity politics has in fact always existed. In the familiar liberal picture, descended from the New Deal, the pressure groups, as they used to be called, were placated one by one, often in ways far more absurd and self-canceling than they are now. The legendary 1947 memo that Clark Clifford, a White House counsellor, sent to Harry Truman (it may have had multiple authors) outlining what was then an improbable path to victory in the presidential election, simply lists all the pressure groups on the Democratic side—farmers, Jews, Negroes, organized labor, Southerners—and explains how to keep them all in your hand without having to discard any, as if playing political gin rummy, a favorite card game of the period. Please them enough, and they would vote. They did. Even if they were appealed to by umbrella themes that spoke to the common good in public, the essential part was pleasing them in private by giving them what they wanted. If this was not identity politics, it is hard to know what is.

So, the trouble is not that identity or pressure group politics are new or alien to liberal democracy, it's that the goal of playing pressure group politics is to build a winning hand. We can ask and even cajole people to extend the rights that they enjoy to others. We can ask them, sometimes successfully, to share instead of hoard—even demand that they do it. That has, historically, been a very successful social project. It is why seven coal miners were in the British cabinet not much more than fifty years after coal miners were allowed to vote. Silencing people, or giving them the strong feeling that they are not being heard at all, is, histor-ically—as marginalized people should be the first to recog-nize—a completely *unsuccessful* social project.

The only problem with identity politics is making sure you have enough identities on hand to make up a genuine politics. Democratic politics are an inclusive arithmetic, or they are nothing. They can never be successful as an exer-cise in excommunications.

So intersectionality seems to come in two versions, one helpful and the other less so. The sophisticated version in-sists that these nodes identify types of difference and with it types of oppression that are invisible to most eyes. (The gay Jews who did so much to make modernism are a good instance of the kind. Being *both* Jewish and gay was a clan-destine truth, central to their predicament and their power; and of course, being both Jewish and gay now is a different collision of kinds, as likely to produce an Internet tycoon as an inspired avant-gardist.) By asking us to see how these social roles intersect in oppressive ways, the new kinds of analysis can open our eyes to hidden truths. The less inter-esting version loses the fluidity of its own social observation and simply turns these intersections into fixed types—not much richer than the astrologer's Libras or Virgos. Weap-onized to assert an unchallengeable authority that derives from a particular identity set, the logical consequence is to make *any* identity set so individual that it leaves you with no authority to speak for anyone other than yourself. (The em-phasis on difference above all else is, as we've seen, a feature of extreme *right*-wing thought in Europe, too.)

We can all speak only for ourselves. But we can all speak *to* as many others as will listen. This asymmetry is what makes public conversation possible. What matters is not who says it but the sanity of what's said.

⁓⟐⁓

Thinking about public arguments and public debate leads us—there's no escaping it—to another stormy issue, that of free speech and its discontents. There's no issue on which liberals and leftists still disagree more profoundly—more radically, if you like—than on the issue of how free speech is and how free it ought to be. The liberal view of free speech comes down to us from that bedrock document, Mill's 1859 "On Liberty." When it comes to free speech, Mill wants us to ask something simple: Is this practice causing me any real harm? Not potential harm to my feelings, not social harm to my idea of right, not damage to the great precepts of religion or to my stuffy uncle's sense of propriety or to my inner sense of safety. Unless the speaker is actually about to cut your throat, you have to let him work his jaw. Mill knew that questions not decidable by proof were still amenable to argument. The authoritarian position is not the strongest one but merely the most frightened. Nothing is worse for being looked at; no idea is good enough to exist unopposed.

For liberals, free speech is a nearly sacrosanct principle and should be curbed only at the absolute extreme. Freedom to criticize without fear is essential to the search for new knowledge, and without new facts—and the new ideas they discipline—we cannot reform our ideas or our behavior. History tells us that today's blasphemy is tomorrow's self-evidence, that the most critical view we speak today may turn out to be tomorrow's wisdom. There should be no more rule by royalty? No more education by the church alone? Well, obviously, these are reasonable views now, even majority ones. But there was a time when you put your very life in jeopardy speaking them. You could be ripped apart limb from limb on a public scaffold for saying so. That time was a preliberal or antiliberal one. We must never return to it.

For the left, on the other hand, free speech is always a subject of power and its invocation frequently a mask for it. The liberal assertion of free speech must never be seen as a value outside the larger context of power: who gets to speak, and how speech is heard, and how pained or threatened the listeners of that speech may feel. Mill's idea of free speech is what we now call elitist or class-bound. He assumes a pleasant argument among gentlemen, or at most gentlemen and gentlewomen. He does not adequately imagine the way that speech is bought and sold to keep the persecuted in their place. He does not know what it really feels like to hear hatred directed at your person or your group. Free speech is fine; freed people are better.

The view that free speech is only one of many competing values that we ought to think about in public debate need not be trivial. One can be an impeccable liberal and still believe in sharp limits to what can be said in public discourse. Another of my liberal heroines, for instance, is Justice Rosalie Abella of the Supreme Court of Canada. The daughter of Holocaust survivors, born in a displaced persons camp in Germany, she came to Canada as a small child and became first a distinguished lawyer and then an even more distinguished judge, without ever losing her common touch and her human warmth—*everyone* calls her Rosie.

But she, while the fiercest of advocates of the independence of the judiciary from political or executive pressure—a
case she has made in Israel as in Canada—is also far from
a free speech absolutist. Canada, as we've seen, was born as
a multicultural country, with great respect paid to the particular exigencies and sensitivities of its two founding people,
English and French—with the First Nations people always a
tutelary presence, if not always treated as such—which then
got extended to all the other immigrant peoples who make
Canada such a shiningly diverse country. (Every morning
on the bus to school, I passed by the Notre-Dame-de-Grâce
kosher delicatessen; no one thought such accidental hy-
brids of religious coexistence even vaguely strange. The
history of Canadian tolerance is not perfect, but it is less
imperfect than that of almost any other country.)

As a consequence, Canadians understand that civil liberties and human rights, far from being a natural consequence of each other, are two forces in frequent tension.
Abella writes that "civil liberties had given us the universal
right to be equally free from an intrusive state, regardless
of group identity; human rights had given us the universal
right to be equally free from discrimination *based* on group
identity." We need both. As she argues and has adjudicated,
we can certainly consider limits on freedom of expression
in the interests of the feelings of a marginalized group: "a
limitation on freedom of expression will only pass constitutional scrutiny if it is a reasonable limit that can be demonstrably justified in a free and democratic society." Hate
speech is a real thing and should be stopped. To take the
most vivid instance, Canada has sturdy laws against hate
speech. Holocaust denial, in the Canadian view, may be

simply a lie, damaging to our memory and an act of deliberate cruelty to those who survived the camps. You can't say it because it isn't true and does harm.

But hate speech law has broader applications. One case, on which the Supreme Court of Canada ruled, was against a Saskatchewan man who had passed out antigay literature, accusing gay teachers of sharing "filth and propaganda" and teaching "sodomy" to their students. Another of his pamphlets showed that the Bible clearly defines homosexuality as "abomination" and that Sodom and Gomorrah were "destroyed by God's wrath" as a result of homosexual "perversion." (In America, these views are commonplace; the pamphleteer could probably get a seat on a federal court.) In Canada, the Supreme Court found that the provincial law that forced him to cease distributing the pamphlets was entirely constitutional. "The objective of preventing the harm to minorities caused by hate speech was sufficiently important to justify limiting freedom of speech, particularly expression of slight social value."

So liberal faith in free speech need not be absolute to remain liberal. Tolerance is a positive virtue, but it has limits—and the limits are damage done to threatened or marginalized people.

This view is, to an American free-speech absolutist, alarming if not anathema. Who are judges to decide what harm can come to a minority? Couldn't the publication of *The Satanic Verses* do similar harm to minorities? One could say in response that that's significant literature, not pamphleteering of "slight social value." Well, who's to decide? a lawyer at the ACLU asks. A judge? A panel of judges? Does history suggest that this is a good guide to enduring value?

The right to mock religion surely cannot be less important than the right of the religious not to be criticized.

At the same time, liberals can understand and recognize that there are many ways in which speech happens. It's well understood that commercial speech is always limited: you can't advertise a cancer cure that doesn't work. And of course, there is the famous line about fire and theaters. You can't speak freely to endanger a life. So it isn't evasive to say that many views are possible on free speech issues and that American absolutism is far from the only truly liberal kind.

But it's also necessary to say that the foundation on which we build ought to be as *close* to absolute as we can make it. The dispositive liberal attitude about the ways in which we can constrain or circumscribe free speech has as its obvious premise that speech should be free. We should do everything we can to reinforce diversity of opinion even as we struggle to assist a diversity of kinds. The leftist or radical view is that freedom of speech is less foundational than the right to protect difference, the right not to feel threatened or aggrieved or set upon, and the right not to have to tolerate intolerable views. The liberal believes that tolerance must be as tolerant as it possibly can be. Freedom of expression is a foundational value to be limited only in extreme circumstances.

The disagreement is real and profound, and the attempts on college campuses to restrain speech are very alarming to liberals exactly because the starting premise does not seem to be free speech first, constrained as necessary, but human rights or social justice first, to be enforced as needed. The radical response, basically, is that right-wing speech doesn't need the support of progressives because it already has the support of Rupert Murdoch. Real though the problem of civil liberties on campuses might be, it is infinitely less concerning than the power of corporate speech or the daily presence of hate speech from the highest source of power directed against threatened groups. College kids in effect egging a professor's door because they don't like what she said is not remotely similar to watching Fox News presenting a steady stream of lies about transgender people and Mexican rapists and the rest. Failing to see this is not to see the world as it really is.

Grown-up people can count to two. Both kinds are wrong. As with everything in human disputes, limitations on speech depend on the particular: we have to look at it case by case and specificity by specificity. Criticism of religious ideologues may be very different than Holocaust denial, even if both are forced under the heading of "hate speech." That there's no escaping the specificities of the world is *the* foundational liberal instinct, even in its way more foundational than freedom of debate. There's no looking past the particulars. We have to make significant minute discriminations between, say, people who are being invited on a college campus simply as a means of provocation and those who are teaching and have a right to unfettered expression even of the most unorthodox opinions. We have to distinguish between genuine hatred directed at an ethnic group and bold blasphemy directed at an ideology. We have to distinguish between insulting someone's beliefs—something none of us enjoy but which all of us have to endure—and threatening someone's safety.

These may seem hard distinctions to make. They often are. But what liberals believe is that parsing particulars is the work of social sanity. The first premise should be plural-ism and tolerance; the last resort should be its repression. A slippery slope? All slopes are slippery. The slippery slope is what Mill called liberty. Every time we slide a little further down, what we have found in the past is not a descent to-ward hell but more air and more people breathing free.

Let's return, though, to where we began, to the question of the Congo and its genocide and liberal responsibility. One reason that liberalism is at a rhetorical disadvantage against leftist radicalism is, simply, that a great deal of the radical reproach to liberalism is *true*, and the best response is to say: You're right. Let's do better. We need to do more. We speak, or try to, in King Lear's words during the storm when he has become aware of the huge range of human suffering to which he had before been blind:

> O, I have ta'en
> Too little care of this! Take physic, pomp.
> Expose thyself to feel what wretches feel,
> That thou mayst shake the superflux to them
> And show the heavens more just.

(Lear on the heath is a radical, raging. We remember that scene clearly. Safer in his little heath-hut, he becomes some-thing more like a liberal.)

Liberalism *is* fallibilism. It does not begin with an un-duly optimistic idea of human nature. Just the opposite—it begins with Montaigne's original understanding that any government, any ruler, any system of order will be flawed, divided, inherently unjust, and incapable of reconciling all sides of its nature. That fallibilism is not something that comes late and reproachfully to the liberal tradition. It is the heart of it. It is why we think of Montaigne as the first real liberal.

This is not just the core conception of liberal humanism. It is the core *competence* of liberal humanism. It is where all that tiresome rules-on-the-back-of-the-box liberal proce-duralism—the insistence on following rules made up to en-sure equal treatment, the waiting-in-line-at-the-DMV side of liberalism—is essential to its task of expressing humane values. They meet in the idea that power cannot control justice. When we have a complaint against the powerful, we can appeal to something like an unbiased institution. The "merely formal" freedoms of the liberal dispensation turn out to be vital for real freedom.

Liberalism makes the idea of fallibility into a political practice by trying not to have too much power concen-trated in one place or part of the system. One reason that pollution was so catastrophically extreme in Eastern Eu-rope is not that corporate capitalism is virtuous and com-mand economies evil. It's that corporate capitalism is still, so far, chained within a liberal society—against its own will, to be sure—and so caught up within the constant feedback processes of public opinion and the liberal courts. You can't get away with everything. In a command economy you can because power, justice, and free speech are regulated by a single system.

It goes without saying that that's a difficult and uncer-tain conception to insist on. But what is astonishing is how much and how often it does work. And it's why the first thing that enemies of liberalism always want to do is take the courts and the justice system under personal or party control. The divisibility of power is the guarantee of protest.

The horrors of colonialism happened and remain a constant reproach to the liberal tradition. That's one reason why compassionate and intelligent people should never be seduced or impressed by anyone who talks about Western values or Western civilization as though this was not a cheap cover for a great variety of enterprises—some impressive, some unimaginably cruel. Western civilization is the Belgian genocide—and indeed the Jewish genocide—just as much as it is Darwin and sewers.

Yet, over the centuries, the fallibilism central to liberalism has sponsored within it a corrective conscience. The atrocities can come from within the liberal order—and so does the urge to correct them. Not just the specific protests but also the idea of protest as a constant living alternative to injustice is a particularly liberal one. It is part of its belief in the constant *necessity* of reform.

The urge to commit atrocities is standard to all human systems; the institutionalized urge to amend them is not. The Catholic Church has to be dragged over centuries to apologize for threatening to torture Galileo—or even today, over decades to confront the nightmare of sexual abuse. It is not that cardinals are worse people than, say, university presidents, it is that they work within a system specifically designed to suppress dissent, extend secrecy, impose hierarchy, and make official sins as discreetly unseeable as possible. The rationale for doing this is clear and, where sincere, even perhaps admirable: bad things done by priests are a "scandal" to the true faith, and since the true faith *is* true, and essential not just to fatten some men's wallets but to save humanity's souls for all eternity, the church would be crazy to allow the fallible habits of one or two hundred clerics to stand in their way. This is, on its own terms, a perfectly consistent belief.

But it is not a liberal one. The old exasperated reproach directed at the liberal—that a liberal cannot even agree with himself—is a sign of the corrective conscience at its constant work. That other contemptuous watchword, *liberal guilt*, is no more than fallibilism making itself felt internally.

For, along with the horrors that liberalism abides or even causes, we find liberal people willing to stand up and say that these *are* horrors. We've already seen one example, when the British Liberal leader Gladstone called out the "Bulgarian horrors," the atrocities committed in the 1870s by the Ottoman Empire, as an issue that mattered to everyone even if the British themselves were not directly responsible for them. Consider, too, the Jamaica revolt of the 1860s, so brutally put down by the British authorities—yet how, while the established power structure supported the cruelty, the leading liberal lights of the day, including Darwin and Mill and Huxley and Leslie Stephen (Virginia Woolf's father), all stood up in protest and demanded that justice be done to the "mutineers" and punishment meted out to the British governor of Jamaica.

The horrific case of the Belgian Congo is similar. The partial remedy for the horror—the call and the awareness against it—came out of the liberal system of self-correction. Let me introduce you to one more liberal of note—ambivalent and double-souled as so many of us are, being human—and that is E. D. Morel. It was Morel, a minor shipping clerk in a Liverpool firm, who saw, in visits to Belgium, a sinister discrepancy between what was being sent to the Congo—guns and ammunition—and what was coming back: rubber and ivory. He made the correct deduction about what this "trade" must mean and began a crusade to expose the Congolese cruelties. In remarkably short order, he refused what was in effect a bribe to keep silent and left the firm to become a journalist, eventually starting his own paper, the *West African Mail*. He pursued the story relentlessly, recruited a remarkably august team of witnesses and writers to his cause, including Arthur Conan Doyle, Joseph Conrad, and Mark Twain—who, in the dark mood that filled his life's end, wrote a bitter satiric monologue, "King Leopold's Soliloquy." Eventually, by 1903, Morel saw a resolution condemning the cruelties pass the House of Commons and then, still later, the formation of a Belgian commission of inquiry, which confirmed all of his reports. The conception of the Congo as a private royal fiefdom of the king, which had allowed the holocaust to happen, was gone. None of it restored the lives or the limbs of those who were killed and mutilated. But far from being covered up and forgotten, it was exposed and revealed by liberal institutions. Too late? Yes, too late. But people saw, and people cried out, and their cries were amplified, not suppressed, by liberal institutions.

Morel went on to behave bravely as an imprisoned pacifist, alongside Bertrand Russell, in the Great War—and then, to our eyes, much less well, when he became a critic of atrocities committed by the French army in the war, which he blamed, oddly, given his courage about the Congo, exclusively on black African troops. Fallibilism is a universal fact. But at the crucial moment, Morel's ability to act and be heard was uniquely possible to a liberal temperament in a liberal state.

What liberalism can say on its own behalf is that no system of power in human history has tried so hard to inject a corrective conscience into its institutions. It is not merely that individuals within liberal societies act against atrocity, but that liberal institutions are there to protect their protests. (Never without difficulty, but, to date at least, pretty much always at the end of the day.) The very fact that the larger left-wing reproach to liberalism is nurtured and sheltered within that quintessential liberal institution, the research university, is not a hypocrisy, as some conservatives still insist, to be apologized for, but a shining specificity, to be praised as an instance of liberal wisdom. The goal of liberal education should always be to make us acutely aware of illiberal acts. That we are now more aware of how many of those have been committed over the centuries by liberalism itself is a positive development, only to be welcomed. One need only compare this process with that of all authoritarian states—where not just the corrective conscience but *all* criticism, including minimal empirical feedback, is forbidden or minimalized—to see why the liberal state can confront and, sometimes, correct its own injustices more rapidly than any other society on the fully historical record.

❧

"OK, fine," I hear an impatient radical interlocutor say again, and again it sounds a bit like you, Olivia: "You simply appropriate the social democratic triumphs for yourself and call them liberalism. That's an easy game to play. Just claim the good stuff for your credo, blame the bad stuff on the next guy's, and shrug and say—when an atrocity your credo made happen gets pointed out—'Well, nobody's perfect!' This is exactly why people hate liberals. They're self-satisfied—smug."

But when liberals take the credit for the accomplishments of the social democratic state—for national health insurance, social security, and the welfare blanket that keeps people comforted, a better term than *safety net*—we're merely being accurate. Social democrats are socialists who saw the liberal light. Can. I make a slightly absurd but apropos analogy? The Byrds were an American rock band from California who were the first to wear long hair, play electric guitars, and have hits with electrified (guitar and bass, plus drums) versions of Dylan songs, including "Mr. Tambourine Man." It was said at the time that they were Dylanized Beatles, but the great rock critic Ellen Willis helped make her reputation by pointing out that they were really Beatleized Dylans—kids from the same background as Dylan who had heard the Beatles and gone electric (as Dylan would himself). It was a crucial point in rock music history. It justified the preference for high pop over folk protest singing. It made pop more urgent. The difference between Dylanized Beatles and Beatleized Dylans seemed small but meant everything.

Similarly, social democrats are not democrats who went socialist, but, historically, socialists who went liberal. In France and England and elsewhere, they struggled and engaged often bitterly and even violently with communist and other far-left groups, rejecting their insistence that only after a revolution and the dictatorship of the proletariat could social justice happen. Instead, the social democrats learned, obeying the rules of parliamentary democracy gave access to social change on a fast track and without the concentration camps and the mass killings. Clement Attlee, the saintly leader of the mid-twentieth-century British Labour Party—saintlier for being entirely sane to the point of complete tedium—rejected communism for parliamentary politics. (He was supposedly the model of the prime minister for whom James Bond worked against SMERSH.) He sat alongside Churchill during the war and supported him unconditionally, then led Labour to power by peaceful means, rejecting every one of Churchill's domestic policies—and resigned when Labour lost the confidence of the country by the same means. Attlee was a socialist-minded politician working resolutely within a liberal frame. Social democracy is a form of adapted liberalism—not surprisingly, since liberalism is an injunction of constant adaptation.

Free-market economics, social democratic liberals have always believed, are an engine of productivity and prosperity; free-market economies, left to their own devices, also invariably first produce prosperity, then inequality, then a bubble, and then the bubble bursts. To use a favorite idiom of mine borrowed from the French, grown-up people should be able to count to two. The challenge is to get the productivity without the explosion, while trying to reduce the inequality. These views are central to the liberal tradition—that's why Mill, who believed so passionately in liberty, also called himself a socialist. Neoliberalism, the bogeyman of the current left, the belief that free-market solutions will solve everything, is a kind of cuckoo child deposited in the liberal nest—sometimes nurtured, certainly, by panicked liberal adoptive parents but not part of the genetic liberal line at all.

The good news is that this challenge is not actually all that big a challenge. Building a perpetual motion machine is a challenge. Building a free-market society with strong social insurance, equality of education, and medical care guaranteed for all—there are lots of very big societies like that. It's not magic. Hundreds of millions of people are citizens of such societies in Europe, Canada, and Australia, not just in the sometimes overly idealized Nordic countries. These societies are themselves imperfect. *All* societies are imperfect. They are capable of being made better—fairer, kinder, more reliable—with the right kind of pressure on the right parliamentary parts. They present problems of their own, but this is not because capitalism is newly in a crisis but because every society is *always* in a state of change, which we can call a crisis in order to make it lurid—presenting problems, of varying degrees of gravity, in need of remedial reform. No imaginable society would not have these characteristics: liberal societies try to bring them forward and address them; authoritarian societies try to disguise or hide them, or when they can't be hidden anymore, find someone else to blame for them. A society, like a weekly magazine, is one long perpetual crisis. Solving this crisis long enough to get to the next one is the work we do.

⁂

It's obvious, I hope, how keenly I admire Emma Goldman as a writer and activist both. But by the latter part of her life, she was so busy bearing witness to the essential truth her leftist compadres didn't want to hear—that the Russian Revolution was a brutal and bloody catastrophe—and so consumed with trying to survive, that she was unable to see what was staring her in the face: that she was able to take refuge in London and later in Toronto, Winnipeg, and Montreal because, as imperfect as these liberal lands were with their many prejudices, they had no instruments of coercion, no single party line or secret police. (America did, sporadically, and it nearly destroyed us. Fortunately, even J. Edgar Hoover, as bad a man in his way as Lavrentiy Beria, was unable to finish off his enemies.)

To use a contemporary locution, Goldman never stopped to "theorize" this discrepancy. The London she fled to eventually after her Russian sojourn was cold and foggy—she evokes it about as well as it could be evoked— but the sounds of dissidents being lined up and shot (the apologists told her that it was students taking rifle practice), which she could hear all night in Moscow, never disturbed the London fog or the Canadian cold. In Montreal and in Toronto, she was not only able to live her life but to lecture on Walt Whitman.

Combining those kinds of civil liberties with a more just economic system was *work*—work being done in those years by actual antiutopian practical politicians, from one end of Canada to the other, who were laying in place the system of social protections that, made more urgent by the cruelties of the Great Depression, evolved and survived to this day. (The most admired Canadian in every poll was, for a long time, T. C. "Tommy" Douglas, the prime minister of Saskatchewan, who brought Medicare for all to Canada.)

Canada, a bourgeois liberal country evolving into a social democracy, held out a warm welcome to an anarchist activist. It was the promised land, though she had suffered so much that she could not entirely understand its promise. Why the American liberals had been panicked into betraying their own principles during the First World War was as good a question to raise as why the Marxists had turned out to have no principles to betray.

But though Goldman could theorize history, she could not theorize her own experience. Molière wrote a comedy about a doctor in spite of himself; Goldman became a liberal in spite of herself, without becoming a conservative to spite the old radical she had been. (Max Eastman, an equally interesting human spirit, did make that move in the end, writing for the *National Review*.) And of course, it hardly needs saying, the Canada she ended in was imperfect—but the flaws, real and in need of remedy, were small and secondary in any decent historical perspective. (Removing aboriginal kids from their homes is wrong; it is not on the same wavelength of wrongness as murdering thousands of dissidents without trial or starving whole nations into submission.)

Liberalism without vision is, indeed, merely comfortable, but radicalism without realism will always be blind—still waiting for the great red hope and then surprised by the next great catastrophe. Radicals who have not learned the necessity of liberal institutions have learned nothing, nothing at all, from history. Emma Goldman was a sterling witness to this cycle who did the bravest thing: she saw what she saw and said what she had seen. But, though keenly conscious of history, she treats the refuges she found as in some way natural, just the way Canada is or London always was, not as places that were the subject of history, and of historical actors, that could have led them in different directions and end in a very different way. Of course! she seems to imply, an anarchist would naturally find safe haven at the end of an agonized world journey not in Germany or Russia but in Toronto and Winnipeg. But this was not just due to what Germany wasn't, but to all that Winnipeg was.

Emma Goldman shows us that radicals who have not learned that liberal institutions are rare and fragile have failed to learn from experience. I fear to hear younger radical-minded people in particular (but older ones have the same predilection) talk about key liberal institutions and practices—the insistence on pluralism, the respect for a free press, the expectation of the oscillation of parties in power—impatiently. They speak as though these institutions and practices are the self-evident ground of social life, ones that can be depended on to renew themselves, or easily reconstructed after a revolution, rather than as the immensely delicate, hard-won, and historically unique things they really are. They were almost impossibly difficult to build, and it would be a crazy defiance of history to think they can easily, or ever, be rebuilt after their destruction. Liberal institutions and practices are fragile. Once broken, they shatter. The contemporary left can sometimes seem to have an insufficient respect for the fragility of the very same liberal institutions that allow its views to be broadcast without impediments. The left makes an unfortunate alliance with right-wing authoritarians when it deprecates those institutions. It does this sometimes with impatience, sometimes with the illusion that things have to get worse before they get better. Marxists called this "heightening the contradictions," that is, making the true nature of capitalism or the social order so oppressive that even previously wishy-washy people will be driven to the barricades.

In truth, the liberal replies, history shows that things that get worse get even worse and go on getting worser. No good has ever come from heightening the contradictions. All that happens is that the institutions get weaker, and authoritarians become stronger in the weakened spaces. Making common cause with conservatives who don't share reformist causes but do share their commitment to liberal institutions such as free speech, the oscillation of power, the right to be heard, the independence of the judiciary—all that's summed up in the simple but revolutionary phrase *the rule of law* rather than of party or dictator—is work that liberals see as essential. Liberals welcome this coalition, without imagining that there is some mysterious third way in which their difficulties and differences would dissolve, because for liberals coalition and compromise are *fighting* words, devices to battle by.

※

But liberals who have not learned to pay attention to the radical cries for justice have learned nothing from history either. Reform is an ongoing process, rarely begun or completed by liberalism alone—at each point a new movement for justice had to arise to occupy parks and chain itself to fences and cross bridges and face down police dogs. This prophetic force is one that liberals should learn from, be open to, and often be humbled by.

We need not look as far as the Congo to see the radical assault on liberal reformism at its work. We need look no further than to the man I think of as perhaps the greatest of all Americans, Frederick Douglass. In his life, we find an almost operatic drama of the permanent struggle between the radical prophet and the liberal politician, made more moving because they were embodied in a single man. In some ways, that struggle can be traced back to the biblical exchange of Moses and Aaron, where the prophetic impatient leader and his brother, the officious high priest, seem to engage in a struggle between principles and pragmatism. The same two archetypes appear again and again in the history of liberalism, and no two more memorably than Frederick Douglass and Abraham Lincoln during that crucial liberal decade of the 1860s.

Lincoln's story has been told so often, and from so many angles, that his legacy is an unquestioned part of the liberal tradition. (Though perhaps the most complicated part of it is that this preacher of binding up wounds and of malice toward none also prosecuted one of the bloodiest and most brutal wars in human history to that point and prosecuted it with a bland acknowledgment that it was a question of human arithmetic—which side had more bodies to sacrifice.)

Douglass is a more complicated case. We know of him as a heroic escaped slave who had defied his brutal master at the knowing risk of his own life, deciding that death was better than continual submission. Two years after his escape, he got a job as a laborer in New Bedford, was brought to an abolitionist meeting in Nantucket, then a booming whaling port, and made an impromptu speech that changed history. He spoke about his life as a slave and his flight, stealing the show and the moment. No one had ever heard an ex-slave speak with such precision and eloquence about his own experiences. White abolitionists, followers of William Lloyd Garrison, pressed him into service as a speaker, and Douglass spent the next fifteen years of his life riding trains from one abolition meeting to the next while Anna, who had come north after him, waited in New Bedford and raised an ever-growing crop of children. (They had five in all, including three sons who served in the Civil War, one of them surviving the massacre of Robert Gould Shaw's regiment at Fort Wagner in South Carolina.)

Like many other young and still unformed activists who discover in themselves a gift for oratory, Douglass had to self-educate even as he was speaking. Young orators' tongues are formed before their minds are set. This happened to Martin Luther King Jr., who had to inhabit a leadership position that he was not yet prepared to fully embody, as it did to Emma Goldman, who became Red Emma almost before she mastered English. (In a more benevolent manner, it's what happened to Barack Obama, one eloquent speech turning him from a young man with little political experience into a plausible presidential candidate, with a steep learning curve to run up.) In each case, the challenge is to keep one's independence, and head, as others are trying to turn you into their megaphone.

Douglass passed from slave to celebrity in about a year and remained one for the rest of his life. He is one of the small list of people who have been, or are, in effect, the *face* of their movement. Gloria Steinem was not the most important feminist thinker of her time, or its most significant organizer, but she was the face of American feminism for a reason. She embodied the reality, confounding to sexists, that a woman who looked like her could be a radical egalitarian about gender. Douglass embodied the reality, confounding to racists, that a black man could be charismatic, eloquent, imposing, intimidating, educated, and a voice for absolute emancipation. He sometimes looks like a fiercer George Washington—Roman nose, fierce blank scowl of virtue, and swept-back classical hair. In a new culture of reproduced images, these things counted.

The story of Douglass's relation to Garrison, as much as his relation to Lincoln, is itself a key story in American political history. Garrison, the most famous abolitionist of the period, had been the top of the bill until Douglass was asked, without warning, to tell the story of his life. Overwhelmed by Douglass's eloquence, Garrison asked the crowd, "Have we been listening to the testimony of a thing, a piece of property or a man?" Douglass went on the road as a Garrisonite, a devotee of Garrison.

But, less than a decade later, they broke, bitterly and for life. Some of the bitterness rose from Douglass's uneasy sense that he was not so much being used as being put on display. But more derived from a decisive intellectual difference, one that still sculpts American politics. Garrison was both a pacifist and a moral secessionist. He believed that the Constitution was so deeply implicated in slavery—including its creation of the small-state-favoring Senate—that it could not be salvaged. Douglass came to believe that the Constitution was in fact a good document gone wrong—that in its democratic premises it breathed freedom and that it needed only to be amended to be restored to its first purposes. Douglass most forcefully offered this insistence, as I've said, in his 1852 Fifth of July speech in Rochester. It is a masterpiece of startling argumentative twists. He begins with unstinting praise of the values and character of the Founding Fathers—the only forewarning of dissent being his speaking of the events of the 1770s in the second person—*your* founders did this, *your* history says that. Then he makes his thundering turn: "The existence of slavery in this country brands your republicanism as a sham, your humanity as a base pretense, and your Christianity as a lie." Finally, he makes a still more surprising swerve, back toward the American center: the Constitution is solid, all that needs fixing is our way of reading it. "Interpreted as it ought to be interpreted, the Constitution is a GLORIOUS LIBERTY DOCUMENT. Read its preamble, consider its purposes. Is slavery among them? Is it at the gate-way? or is it in the temple? It is neither." (I've quoted these words before, but I'll quote them again. They count for a lot.)

The constitutional issue was, and remains, epic. All of American liberalism remains at stake in this choice. It is what divides Obama from Cornel West and his other critics on the left. For Garrison, the failure of liberal constitutionalism to achieve its stated aim was a reason to abandon it. For Douglass, the failure of liberal constitutionalism to achieve its stated aim was a reason to restate the aim more forcefully and more inclusively. If the aim was in the document, the arc could yet be completed. He thought the aim was there, and the arc was possible.

At the same time, Douglass's belief in the integrity of the American Constitution made him less willing to wait for legislative remedies and readier to use violence against the slave establishment. This became Lincoln's reasoning, too, evident in his legendary speech at Cooper Union in 1860: the historical evidence showed that the signers of the Constitution considered slavery a national question, up for national debate. It wasn't a local or states' rights question. Wrongly decided once, it was still on the agenda of the nation as a whole. Slavery was, in the name of the Constitution, to be assaulted frontally. (How frontally Lincoln could not decide, until events overtook him as president.)

In the early years of the war, Douglass was the model of a radical prophet confronting a timid liberal politician. Lincoln's timidity, his apparent readiness to search for a compromise with the South, or even his insistence that he was fighting for the Union, not specifically against slavery, let alone his willingness to entertain projects of repatriation of the slaves to Africa or elsewhere, disgusted Douglass (whose mind had been shaped by the European romantics). This was liberalism at its worst, looking for a deal with the devil even when the devil wasn't dealing. "We are not to be saved by the captain, but by the crew," he aphorized—meaning by the army, not the commander.

But as the war went on, Douglass came to understand and empathize and even identify with Lincoln's struggle as he understood it more clearly. Lincoln, who hated slavery with his heart and soul, still had to bring on not merely Douglass's allies or his people but a broad coalition of Northerners who, though hardly friendly to slavery, still had to be persuaded to allow their sons to die for its elimination. Some of the northern whites, never let it be gainsaid, really were heroes of altruistic righteousness. The Shaws and Higginsons, Massachusetts-born men who led black regiments, were acting on abolitionist principle alone. They didn't have to fight; they didn't have to lead; little personal gain or glory accrued to them in their lifetime by their actions. They did what was right.

But for the most part families in Ohio and Illinois had to be persuaded that their boys were being sent to die for a cause they could understand, not a remote altruistic one for a people that they might sympathize with but they could not yet identify with (if indeed they ever could). Douglass came to understand that Lincoln had wrapped the right cause around the wrong cry from the best of motives. We still do not appreciate how much the greatness of the Gettysburg Address as a forensic argument lies in the way Lincoln made the two causes—nationalism and emancipation—seem one. The nation was born in the view that all men are created equal; slavery denies that view. If we lose the war then it shows the world that a nation with that premise cannot survive unfragmented. Therefore, fighting for the Union is the same thing as fighting for its first principles. Douglass admired the somewhat sophistic logic. He began impatient and mistrustful of Lincoln, became somewhat more empathetic with his political struggles, and ended a full-hearted admirer, enthralled by the intended scope of the Emancipation Act. Lincoln, for his part, came to understand that Douglass's moral vision was impeccably correct—and a critical undergirding for Lincoln's increasingly militant views. At the second inauguration, Lincoln sought out Douglass at the White House reception and greeted him not as "Mr. Douglass" but as "my friend."

Douglass's political life after the war's end and Lincoln's assassination may seem anticlimactic, and yet in many respects it is as important as what came before. He became, in one view, a conventional party politician, a pillar of the Republican Party. But there is a more positive light in which to see this migration away from militancy. Douglass himself was deeply affected by Lincoln's example of the power of liberal party politics to make real change happen. He became a leader of a party that was, in many respects, an assemblage of minorities and progressives and city people (and neoliberals) gathered in one baggy grouping, not too unlike what we find in the Democratic Party today. Even as Reconstruction failed and Jim Crow overtook the South—a reality that Douglass spoke up against with the same passion that he had spoken against slavery—he devoted most of his time to the construction of black institutions. He helped build colleges; there was also a Freedman's Savings Bank that, sadly, failed after he had agreed to run it. He received (to the dismay of many African American contemporaries) a straight patronage post, as a U.S. marshal of Washington, D.C., in which role he was not above passing along a bit of juice to his friends and, particularly, to his large and not entirely happy family. Having begun as a model of the prophetic kind, he passed, with surprising passion, to become a contented and active party politician, trying to build social capital through intermediate institutions.

Douglass fascinates us because he embodies all the contradictions not just of the black experience in America but more broadly of the radical experience in liberal democracies. Douglass can readily be seen as the father of the most militant strain of resistance, the kind that insists on the uncompromising rejection of racism and on a relentless depiction of its evils, with violence as a recourse when necessary. He believed in violent rebellion, even at times futile rebellion, when the face of racism became intolerable: his seemingly suicidal confrontation as a young man with a brutal slave-breaker is still a model of manhood, self-assertion at the price of possible death. His sense of moral absolutism was completely vindicated by history. No sane person ever doubts any longer that the Civil War had to be an abolition war and only made sense on those terms. The radical reading was the right reading.

But his understanding of pragmatic democratic action taken on a broad front with many allies was vindicated by history too. He was the progenitor and father of the pragmatic-progressive strain that leads directly to Bayard Rustin—disabused of illusions but insistent that the Constitution can be realized in its fullness over time and that democratic politics are the way to do it. This Douglass is the friend of Lincoln, the man who sustained the necessary relations with institutional power—as Dr. King would do, however guardedly, with Kennedy and then with Johnson.

The liberal tradition, of which Lincoln is the great saint, and the radical tradition, of which Douglass is the greatest American instance, are entwined, entangled, braided one into the other. And, on the whole, it is the liberal political practices that proved most potent, most able to constitute an alliance for the Constitution that could win the necessary battles in peacetime and wartime alike. Douglass was a prophetic absolutist *and* a political constitutionalist, and the almost unimaginable bravery of his journey should remind us that both are essential. His heroism lay in being able to embody radical prophet and liberal politician in a single arc of purpose and in one mind and body. Both lives matter.

A THOUSAND
SMALL SANITIES

ELLFLEET, THE LITTLE Cape Cod town where we've been renting a place for three weeks in August for the past thirty-plus years, is, I think you'd agree, a true liberal hotbed. I mean, it's a liberal hotbed in the way that Trollope's cathedral towns were religious hotbeds—the people there may not be able to articulate the principles, but God knows they live the faith. There are yoga studios everywhere you look—at least six by my count. There are Bernie Sanders stickers on bumpers—more than you *can* count. There is a former Zen monk who doubles as a therapeutic masseuse. There is a center for the study of gestalt therapy, and there are six or seven progressive churches. There are farmers' markets, several of them, each for one of the little towns along the Upper Cape—though, suspiciously, exactly the same "farmers" seem to attend the Wellfleet farmers' market as you see at the Truro and Orleans ones, and a lot of what they sell, like kombucha and peach pie, doesn't seem to be particularly local or very farm grown. At each farmers' market, there's a pickup guitar and banjo band of very old guys playing Grateful Dead songs who once were very young guys playing Grateful Dead songs. We attend hand-wringing protest meetings at the library—as a summer town, we're very much out there, against nuclear war—and head-shaking chamber music in the church. There's even the house where the great critic Edmund Wilson, one of my literary heroes, spent his later adult life. Someone is said to have named a brand of Massachusetts medical cannabis in his honor. All the signs of liberal comity, in all its absurdity and all its humanity, are present.

Most of the crises of the liberal order and liberal state in America are felt there, too—we talk about getting away to be more isolated, but we can't escape. Public life is just other people. Politics is just people plus still other people. What was once a working-class community with a summer addition of writers and artists—and the psychoanalysts who attended on them—is now an ever-more stratified one-percenters' place. Rents go up, until only the upper uppers can afford them, the middle-class kids can't, and the working-class locals get thrust farther down the Cape, away from home toward the squatter and more suburban towns. The fried clam stands and the sheds selling vast arrays of brightly colored plastic dinosaur and dragon floats, which once made Route 6 seem still so Patti Page and class-catholic, are vanishing. It's a largely segregated world. Though French Canadians, among whom I grew up, come south in ever greater numbers, their tangy acid French resonating along the beach, black people even from Boston don't. The help in the fried clam shacks and cinnamon bun bakeries, which once was made up of earnest local college kids who put the names of their autumn schools on the tip jar, is all foreign and imported now: Bulgarian and Irish youths who work cheap (do they know the hours they're in for when they take the sweet-sounding jobs?). They have no tip jar for college.

Worse, something has, summer after summer, brought the great white sharks in ever tighter to the shore, so that going to our favorite beach now is a little like taking a hike in a park where tigers lurk. It's still lovely, but—there are tigers. Last summer, we saw a man being carried away and up the dune in a bloody sling, like Jesus in a baroque deposition from the cross, after being assaulted by a shark on Longnook Beach. A week later, right outside our windows, a swimmer was killed, eaten, bitten right in half while he short-boarded.

Rather absurdly, but significantly, wildly divergent right-wing and left-wing explanations of the coming of the sharks are available: the right wing insists that it is a tragedy of exactly that liberal passion for reform that I've been praising, that liberal passion for legislating to improve things in need of no improvement: after the passage of a pious law protecting gray seals from the fishermen who always found them a nuisance, they have now become, as one longtime Cape resident said to us, "ocean rats," and their presence brings the sharks in to shore to eat them and then to eat the people who swim alongside the seals, a classic case of the unanticipated ugly consequences of "reform." The left side insists, just as loudly, that the larger inexorable force of man-made climate change is what's driving both sharks and seals—and the entire ocean ecology—ever farther north and ever more haywire. It's a classic left/right argument: the perils of reform against the horrors of human greed. The stratifications of economic inequality, the ongoing segregation of American life, the presence of immigrant labor for menial jobs and the stresses that creates on both sides, the economic horror, the environmental disasters—you can escape Manhattan, but you can't escape reality. Or other people—plus still other people. Or people arguing over why sharks are eating more other people than they used to.

Of course, we're lucky—privileged, indeed, blessed by good fortune—to have these retreats at all, though we have to work harder every year to make it possible. As I've said, what America has turned into privilege are the minimal comforts that should be guaranteed to all. Read nineteenth-century memoirs, and ordinary clerks and scriveners all have their families disappear for the entire summer to a cooler climate—for that matter it was still a middle-class norm in the 1950s and the comic premise, the whole starting situation, for *The Seven Year Itch*. Beach and lake and mountain holidays are, or ought to be, a human right. In France, Léon Blum and the national Popular Front government legislated for a three-week vacation for *all* French people, a law that still stands firm, emptying Paris out in August, uppers and middles and working class alike.

But then there's that sign that you and I, Olivia , bike by most mornings on Cahoon Hollow Road. It's in front of, yes, a yoga studio, and the owners of the studio put it up this year. It bears a series of political declarations in multi-colored block letters, the rainbow hues carrying a message of their own:

IN THIS HOUSE WE BELIEVE THAT:
BLACK LIVES MATTER
WOMEN'S RIGHTS ARE HUMAN RIGHTS
NO HUMAN IS ILLEGAL

SCIENCE IS REAL

LOVE IS LOVE

KINDNESS IS EVERYTHING.

"Dad, there's your *entire book!*" you said delightedly when we biked past it one day. I think you were delighted that my summer literary labors, once again, were proving all for naught.

You're right—that's a liberal catechism. All the slogans and one-sentence attitudes that comic-book liberals like me are supposed to share. But the more we examine it, the more we see that it also unconsciously captures the dilemma of the liberal imagination. Summoning up in neat capsule form the slogans, the *words*, of liberalism, it actually suggests the *work* of liberalism. Work still undone, yet to be finished. It's a catechism, yes—but not yet a credo.

For some of what it offers are political statements that we can certainly derive from liberal principles and our tradition of political practice. That women's rights are human rights—that's what John Stuart Mill and Harriet Taylor were thinking in front of the rhino's cage. That black lives matter is what thrust Frederick Douglass and, yes, Lincoln, too, through the mud and blood of the Civil War. No human is illegal? That speaks to the inclusion of immigrants that let your grandparents into America—and to the cold refusal that kept other relatives out, Jewish refugees driven to Cuba or South America. And to the even darker history that expelled Emma Goldman. No human ought to be illegal or unwelcome.

"Science is real." Well, even if we know that the description of the Enlightenment as a one-way progressive movement is a caricature of a much-more complicated history, still, we say, yes, argument from evidence, probing for weakness in our own pet theories, the corrective of conscience common to biology and journalism—that is surely part of what liberals believe. Certainly, *science* has been a holy word in my family; to be or become a scientist (four of your aunts are, as is your grandmother) is the highest calling, a lot higher than miscellaneous essayist.

But then we come to the last two claims: that love is love and that kindness is everything. They're true. Entirely true. (The Beatles say so, which ought to be proof enough.) But I know this sets both our minds a little askance. For though they join on seamlessly as a catechism should, they don't *really* follow from the other immediately adjacent all-caps truth, that science is real.

For this—and if I stop my bike to point this out, sapiently, you are right to laugh, but still, listen—is a classic is/ought problem. I mean by that the classic philosophical objection that no *is*—no fact about the world—can make an *ought*, a decision to act in one way or another. This principle is sometimes called Hume's guillotine because it was first clearly articulated by that sympathetic liberal visionary David Hume, and once again, his liberal vision had more to do with being skeptical about what even scientific knowledge can give you than it did with being too trusting in it. He made the emphatic point that religious thinkers especially tended to sneak to an *ought* from an *is*. Writing that "instead of the usual copulations of propositions, *is*, and *is not*, I meet with no proposition that is not connected with an *ought*, or an *ought not*. This change is imperceptible; but is, however, of the last consequence." (By "last consequence" Hume means what we mean by first consequence, that is, the greatest possible consequence. *Liberal* is not the only word that's changed meanings over the centuries.)

Sometimes this is called the fact/value distinction, which may be clearer, but whatever you call it, it's at the heart of the liberal idea of freedom. It may be a *fact* that men and women are physically different but that doesn't mean that they should be *treated* differently before the law. The *value* of equality is independent of the *fact* of physiology. Men may be bigger and stronger than women, but that doesn't mean they ought to be free to dominate them. (They won't in any case, but they shouldn't anyway even if they could.) It may be a fact that animals have always eaten other animals—but that doesn't mean that it's *right* for human beings to slaughter pigs for food. We can hold the value of ending needless suffering for all sentient beings independent of our power to raise and kill lambs. Any human being *is* certainly bound to die—that doesn't mean that we ought not try to cure his cancer. (Philosophers have been arguing endlessly over these questions, and a lot of liberal philosophers think you *can* get from an is to an ought, or from a fact to a value, but usually they just mean that you can get there if you have a very good argument for getting there. Hume's point was that you should avoid just *gliding* there, "imperceptibly.")

And so: We could believe in women's full humanity and still be eager to enlist their intelligence in a reactionary cause. We could believe black lives matter and still think love or kindness is overrated, that only militancy matters. I've been saying since the beginning that liberal humanism is a whole, and it is. But it is a whole because we have *made* it a whole, and it can only continue to be a whole if we go on doing it. That's the liberal task, the liberal project, the liberal preoccupation. Humanism may historically precede liberalism—but liberalism can't mechanically produce humanism. It's a task of mental effort, adjusted to new circumstances. The reality of science doesn't guarantee the primacy of love. What science shows us is the world as it is. We choose to make the world as we want it.

How *do* we get from liberal rationality to liberal morality, from "science is real" to "love is love"? The honest answer is that we can't—not by any single or simple rule. Liberal reasoning is an ongoing, surprising, vigilant *action*. It isn't a deduction from first principles. You can't say, oh, science or God or nature proves that liberalism is right. The most you can say is that experience suggests that treating both the proposition that love is good and the proposition that the facts can be found as true tends to make more people happy. It works. As a pragmatist philosopher would say, it has cash value in the real world. That's what makes liberalism, to my mind, uniquely demanding. It doesn't give you the answers in advance. It makes you take the test, over and over.

❧

In keeping with the notion of the liberal task, I won't resist a pragmatic action—a series of injunctions to make liberalism live again—of my own. I do have that thing every "thoughtful" journalist, and editor, wants—a Positive Program. I mentioned at the start Lewis Carroll's "The Hunting of the Snark" and how the left-liberal is like Carroll's Snark and the neoliberal like his Boojum. Well, let me continue to pay homage to that great poem, where all the characters have names that begin with *b*, by having all my desires for liberalism begin with *p*. (Remembering that other *p*'s—prosperity, pluralism, peace—are the liberal attainments.) Liberalism is a self-critical practice, and it would be crazy to pretend that the present crisis of liberalism isn't in part self-made. If there are misunderstandings or misperceptions, we're responsible for them, and we have to own them and cure them if we can.

If there are three chief injunctions we need to practice, if there is work to do to reconnect liberal practices with moral values, they might be these: Liberalism has become passive, planetary, and private. It needs to become passionate, patriotic, and public-minded. Or rather, liberalism has allowed itself to be *seen*, including by us liberals ourselves, as private, planetary, and passive; it needs to once again reappear in its truer colors as public-minded, patriotic, and passionate.

Liberalism has become privatized in the straightforward sense that too many liberals have too often come to believe that private enterprise is intrinsically better than public enterprise. To the degree that something called neoliberalism ever existed at all, it reflected this undue confidence, born in the middle of the last century and then reinforced by the end of the Cold War, that free-market solutions are always the best solutions. I think that this is a libel on liberalism's best instincts, but no honest liberal can deny that it contains some truth.

Some truth, but not a whole truth. There's nothing in the liberal tradition that makes us believe that private enterprise is necessarily better than common public goods. Scale changes sanity. We all have to distinguish between models (fixed blueprints for the one best kind of political economy) and modalities (changing and mixed systems responding to the needs of the moment). God knows Adam Smith did. Some parts of social life—medical insurance, pensions for the elderly, subsidies for the arts and parks—demand a model operated by all on behalf of all, that is, by the government, in Lincoln's wonderful definition of why governments exist, "to do for a community of people, whatever they need to have done, but cannot do, at all, or cannot, so well do, for themselves in their separate, and individual capacities."

Other parts do far better when left to largely unsupervised entrepreneurial energies. One only has to compare the development of the Internet in America with the paralysis of the top-down Minitel model in France, which created countless small white elephants on the counters of countless apartments as it became plain that the favored technology of the French state was defunct in advance.

And to this add the truth that in the real world it will be impossible to separate government preferences from entrepreneurial energies, self-organizing market forces. The Internet grew up with enormous help from the U.S. Defense Department, and almost all of the American free market is shaped by, and for, big businesses through government intervention. We can be in favor of humanizing work by putting workers on company boards without being in favor of command economies and five-year plans.

It's a muddle. Liberals like muddles. Liberalism ought to be agnostic about these modes, investing no religious significance in any one. To deny that capitalism left to its own devices produces bubbles, busts, and brutal human inequalities is to deny the achingly obvious truth of modern history; to deny that free-market economies have produced prosperity unparalleled in human history—and continue to lift more people out of poverty than any other model known to man—is to deny the thunderously plain. Two things can often be true at once. Two things are *always* true at once. Indeed, if you know only two true things about a social phenomenon, you're not looking, or counting, closely enough.

A New Yorker need only look at his city now to see the ugliness of capitalism, with the oligarch's erection rising in the mid-distance; a New Yorker need only look at his city through time to recognize the miraculous effect of self-organizing forces making streets and corners and the beautiful unpredictable bumping-into of city life. Coming home on a summer morning, we see both. To see one or the other alone is not to see at all. As Montaigne wrote, we must accept that we are double in ourselves and be able to count to two.

What modern liberalism seeks—and needs to be seen to seek—is not a middle way but a *distinct* way, one in which some parts of social life are safely sealed off from the market and other parts are market centered, and these choices are made by us all through democratic means. This is not some utopian nostrum or pious hope. It's a real path, already largely accomplished for millions of people, and capable of being accomplished again. It is a positive path to be positively enjoined, not a middle way to be weakly gestured toward.

We need to become public-minded in other ways, too—and not in politics alone or most of all. We're all inclined to put the well-being of our families ahead of that of all others. It's why I'm talking this book out to you. But I'm writing to a lot of other, less lucky kids too. There is no more important piece of public-mindedness that liberalism needs to recommit to than public education. Almost all of the social advances that liberals take credit for are either the direct result of, or deeply tied to, a system of public education.

I speak to that out of deepest personal experience. My grandfather was a wise and lovely man—I wish you'd known him; three-quarters of my jokes that you sigh at were his—but he was an immigrant with an eighth-grade education, finished at fifteen. (In old photos, all the eighth-graders in his class look forty.) He read and wrote, sort of. My father went to a Philadelphia public school where he had teachers with doctorates and became the sports editor of a thriving daily paper and was able to go on to the University of Pennsylvania, which he was able to "work his way through"—actually paying a full Ivy League tuition with part-time and summer jobs—to become (improbably, though of course I took it for granted growing up) a professor of English literature and an expert in the prose of Samuel Richardson and Samuel Johnson and all the other great masters of Augustan, Christian, and English writing. My mother's story was even more improbable. She came from an even poorer family, and though she got a scholarship, she was turned down for a major in the math department as a woman (a common occurrence at the time). She went into the then new field of research-based cognitive linguistics, where she became a genuinely famous scientist. That's what public education can accomplish in two generations.

Higher education now often seems to be more of a status contest than a means for social ascent. I'm sure the numbers of underprivileged kids getting first-class educations are comparable now as then, but there's no question that the feeling has reinstated itself that universities are designed for elite self-perpetuation. And, as we've learned, emotions matter as much to social life as empirical data. Nowadays, Penn is a destination school that your friends compete for, and though of course you can still win a scholarship, gaining entry certainly feels more difficult and the space between the educated elite and the great mass of ordinary people larger. The ascension by education happens sometimes, still, but it ought to happen always, or as near to always as humanly possible.

Public-spirited means turning the investment we make in education upside down, doing less to add to the massive endowments of already overendowed universities and recognizing what every study shows—that very early education matters most. Preschools and kindergartens are the places where distances can be most effectively annihilated. Everywhere they've been tried, they have a salutary effect not just on the kids' immediate lives but on the long-term inequality gaps in the societies they live in. A vast social investment in early education is the best weapon against inequality and class stratification. And it isn't that hard to accomplish. It is exactly the closest thing we have to a "cholera cure" for our time, a form of public sanitation directed to a big fix through a small sanity.

⤳◈⤲

And then liberalism has become *passive*, inasmuch as our tradition leads us to believe in proceduralism—in the neutral rules alone. No-drama Obama might have used a little bit more. The technocratic cast of character, the analytic temperament, is doubtless admirable for solving political problems when they are imagined as challenges in resource management. But—and this is as true of Macron in France as of Obama here—the technocratic style is plainly inadequate in power.

We have to believe in passionate policies, passionate in their affirmation of values and principles—with the obvious additional corrective that those passions are not in themselves a *replacement* for politics, since the next guy's or girl's countervailing passion will step in to intrude. Other people have equal passions that need to be respected. But the difference between centrists and liberals is that centrists emphasize the difficulty of these choices, while liberals emphasize their simplicity.

There's a simple choice between a society with many gun massacres and a society with few or none; a simple choice between a society with mass poverty and one without; a choice between a society where no one goes bankrupt when Dad has a heart attack and one where that is a constant fear for the middle classes. These are not hard choices, as the centrists say; they are easy choices. They are just choices that have to be made. Getting them made is hard because the self-evidence of even self-evident moral propositions is not immediately evident to every self. That's the work that liberals have to do.

Liberals should never be arrogant, but they should never be apologetic either. Scientific reasoning can't give you values. But once you choose your values, it *can* give you lots of useful truth. There's really an awful lot of stuff about life now *known* that once was not.

We know how to provide national health insurance without overrationing medicine or bankrupting the society—it happens every day in Canada and France and Germany. We know how to end gun violence—Australia did it, neatly and essentially overnight. We certainly know how to end an epidemic of crime without incarcerating everybody. Really *know*. More people ought to know it, too. Higher education should not belong to an elite, and the education of the public should not be seen as an elitist activity.

❧

The one central truth liberals know is that effective reform almost never happens as the result of big ideas sweeping through the world and revolutionizing life. Whenever we look at how the big problems got solved, it was rarely a big idea that solved them. It was the intercession of a thousand small sanities. A thousand small sanities are usually wiser than one big idea.

This was true about the end of the crime epidemic in America. It was true about ending cholera in nineteenth-century London. It was true about universal medical insurance in all the Western countries. It didn't happen all at once but by incremental measures.

Scientific ideas themselves can be amazing and revolutionary, but they have no effect without the support of their own numerable sanities. Darwin wasn't Darwin because he had a big idea. Others had had versions of his great idea before him. He was Darwin because he spent ten years looking for disconfirming evidence and finding the smallest of instances, from pigeon breeding to the passage of seeds in bird's gullets, to show he might be right.

Indeed, the very basis of the genetic variation that Darwin rightly identified as the key to his theory—he didn't know there were genes, but he knew that traits were hereditary—turns out to be another variant of the same truth. The more that biologists look at the behavior of our genome, the more unlikely the old image of single genes turning on single traits, like a light switch turning on the light in a living room, turns out to be true. Instead, not one nor even a hundred but multiple genes, perhaps the entire genome, contribute even to simple-seeming diseases. Even when it comes to the light switch on the living-room wall, a moment's thought shows that it is merely the tail end of an immensely complex system of exchanges that may begin with a distant hydropower plant in Quebec. The light switch turns on the light, but it is the final point of causality, not the first cause.

An infinity of small effects is what makes us human and makes us distinct individuals. And what is true for us as individual cases is true for us as social animals. It's always a lot of stuff happening at once that makes this one thing happen. Liberalism is the social instantiation of this simple observation.

Big ideas are dramatic, borne to us by flights of unicorns. Sane ideas are often a sequence of smallness, rooted up in the mud by rhinos. There was no miracle cure for crime, just the intercession of . . . those thousand smaller sanities. An epidemic of violence was resolved without addressing what were thought to be its underlying disorders. We cured the crime wave without fixing "the broken black family," that conservative bugaboo. For that matter, we cured it without greater income equality or, truth be told, even remotely solving the gun problem.

Even the problem of income inequality may be susceptible to straightforward solutions. Surprisingly small changes in inheritance taxation, for instance, can have vast effects on who owns how much. Liberals might believe in nearly complete inheritance taxation as a social good, reducing the store of inherited wealth, but even very small changes can have huge effects on social inequality. We don't have to burn down the house to punch a skylight in the ceiling. The light gets in that way, too. A strong argument can be made—Andrew Carnegie himself made it—for a 100 percent inheritance tax on the grounds that any good that can be done by money should be done within a lifetime, and the social damage of having a caste of inherited wealth is too large for any good it does. But this is probably an unrealistic proposal, and the good news is that a relatively small change can have a large effect. As Frank Cowell of the London School of Economics has shown, "inheritance taxation at very modest rates can restrain the growth of wealth inequality or reduce the equilibrium level of inequality."

We don't need to know everything, or understand the entire system, to know enough to fix it. We don't need to ask what ultimate fairness would be like to make life fairer now. We have curbed crime without knowing how we did it, simply by doing it in many ways at once. Social cohesion and the sympathy that rises upward from civil society, from things as simple as safer playgrounds and thriving cafés, have turned out to be a miraculous glue for cities and societies—a kind of humanist miracle, really, a lesson about the self-organizing and, sometimes, self-healing capacities of human communities that's as humbling, in its way, as any mystery that faith can offer.

Epidemics seldom end with miracle cures. Most of the time in the history of medicine, the best way to end disease was to build a better sewer and get people to wash their hands. We could end cholera—as they did in London in the 1860s—without really understanding how cholera bacteria work. Chipping away at a problem is usually the very best thing to do; keep chipping, and eventually, you get to its heart.

Liberty's light beams out from her lamp, in the great republican statue in particular, in its particularities, its particles—infinite gradations of radiance, a flood of illumination at once encompassing and specific. Liberty in liberal imagery is a field of energy, which makes us see all that's there around us. (By the way, since I know you have a taste for semicosmic puns, did you know that the first fully realized theory of electromagnetism—of light, like liberty, as a field emitted, as we know now, by countless particular waves—was published by James Maxwell exactly in our magic year of 1865?)

We can be passionate about this incrementalist truth because it embodies big values. Liberal values are positive values: not a passive acceptance of values there already. Invariably, people of faith treat the values of secular and scientific communities as though they were nonvalues—as though the children of reason and reform were living in a world starved of values and making up for the absence by material pleasures. As though the liberal is technological man or scientific man, at best. Liberalism, in this view, is made in the absence of values.

In fact, it's made through alternate values, which in many respects are demonstrably superior values, at least if we believe that the test of a value is its real consequences—the value of skepticism about authority, the value of pluralism, the value of constant small amelioration, the value of compassion instilled as a legal conception. These are positive values that have had a very haphazard existence, historically speaking, but whose consequences are wholly positive. Skepticism about received authority brings us scientific advance—the open-ended hows and whys—and with it the end of plague and famine. Tolerance brings you an absence of massacre and countermassacre; pluralism allows people to live in peace and plan for their children. It means that Orthodox Jews can live alongside faithful Muslims in one neighborhood in Brooklyn, without often coming to blows and, with a secular police presence, never going to war. Making love rather than war turns out to be a sound idea for social policy.

Skepticism, constant inquiry, fallibilism, self-doubt—these don't mean not knowing. They mean knowing more all the time. All of the consequences of these values seem "merely" material, but they are what enable us to live a richer life, accept our mortality, and find the path to unselfish attainment. They allow us to pass on a better world to our children—to spend every day, as Mill and Taylor would have wanted, with better music, more poetry, better food, better wine grown in more places. To make love with whom we want instead of with whom we're ordered. These are positive values. And to those who don't find them satisfying we say: go, choose your own. Liberal tolerance includes tolerance of nonliberals and antiliberals as long as they accept the rules of pluralism. If they find that an intolerable imposition, then, yes, we have a fundamental disagreement that cannot be halved.

✦

And then, liberals have become planetary. We think in a global way. We feel at home in the world. This is an extraordinarily positive idea for so many—it's an extension of liberal cosmopolitanism.

But we can't ignore or look past the profound reality that human beings live in *places*. We can't fix the world around us by looking past the room we're in because the world begins in that room. The world is *made* of rooms—the world is the room, times many millions. Which doesn't mean we shouldn't be busy fixing and healing the world. It just means that real changes begin in our minds and in our immediate daily practices. That's a commonplace not just among quiet, inward-turning contemplative types; it's what every successful social agitator preaches as well. The change has to begin at home, or nowhere.

But rooms reside in places, and a liberal love of place is simply what we mean by patriotism. There's never been a more urgent moment to underline the difference between patriotism and nationalism. One ally in this endeavor is, once again, a novelist, not a pundit or scholar. Philip Roth spent most of the last few years of his (supposedly) silent "retirement" brooding hard on the question of patriotism. A critic of America who nevertheless loved it, he traced his own sense of patriotic feeling back to his school years in Newark, New Jersey, and then to his experience of the much-maligned regionalist writers of the thirties and forties.

"Through my reading, the mythohistorical conception I had of my country in grade school—from 1938 to 1946—began to be divested of its grandiosity by its unraveling into the individual threads of American reality—the wartime tapestry that paid moving homage to the country's idealized self-image," he said. "Reading them served to confirm what the gigantic enterprise of a brutal war against two formidable enemies had dramatized daily for almost four years to virtually every Jewish family ours knew and every Jewish friend I had: one's American connection overrode everything. One's American claim was beyond question. . . . The American adventure was one's engulfing fate." Making the point that he is a particularist and a patriot, at the same time—that only by having a deep local sense of place can one have a larger loyalty that contains within it the necessary contradictions and limits—he both narrowed his own allegiances to working-class Newark and made Newark a microcosm of America. Roth called this, in the final summation of his life's work, "the ruthless intimacy of fiction." He insisted that "this passion for specificity, for the hypnotic materiality of the world one is in, is all but at the heart of the task to which every American novelist has been enjoined since Melville and his whale and Twain and his river: to discover the most arresting, evocative verbal depiction for every last American thing." The job is to be attached to a place as one is attached to a self: not looking past its flaws but literally unable to imagine life without it.

Roth's patriotic proposal invests not in the arc of history but in a more fully realized sense of simple belonging. He proposed a patriotism of place and person rather than of class and cause. His was a patriotism that recognizes, in a classic mode of liberal thought, how helplessly dependent we are on a network of associations and communal energy, of which we become fully aware only as it disappears. Not only *can* you go home again, Roth insists. You can *only* go home again. You get America right by remembering Newark as it really was.

You cannot produce a program for patriotism. But you can *permit* a program of patriotism. The former French prime minister Manuel Valls puts it simply for his country: The left invented Marianne, the symbol of the French Republic, as the left invented the Tricolor, the French flag. It is insane to leave them as symbols to be picked up by the ethnic-nationalist National Front.

❧

Mentioning the National Front reminds me that I've tried to stay away from obvious contemporary political issues— partly because there's a lot of that already and more because things can change so quickly. I wanted to offer something more permanent. The greatest vice of political pundits is presentism: whatever happens now is going to keep on happening. If the Obama coalition is in the ascendant, that's what will continue to ascend; if liberalism is on the rise globally in the early 1990s, it's the end of history. Now, we live on the crest of a populist wave, an illiberal tsunami, that country by country seems likely to sweep away institutions and norms that not long ago seemed stable and bring us all to the condition of Putinism.

Someone once said that we all have the philosophy of our insomnia, meaning that the things that keep us awake at three in the morning are the things we really care about. I'm kept awake at night by the thought that liberal cities and liberal civilization really could disappear, be crushed, and the values built there eradicated, not just curbed. I don't mean to minimize that risk—that's the philosophy of *my* insomnia, that anxiety, the possibility of that disappearance. We've seen in the past two years how easily one petulant autocrat can spit on hundreds of years of democratic predicates and premises. Dark ages happen. But I also don't want to overrate this threat. And the one thing that seems necessary to say, vehemently and clearly, against the whole grain of deep political explication is that I think it is a huge mistake to make these questions too narrowly causative. Populism is on the rise because of immigration; authoritarianism is on the rise because of economic anxiety; authoritarianism is on the rise because of neoliberalism. Not that these things don't contribute—obviously in complicated ways they do. But these problems are permanent. These passions—the desire for simplicity, the hunger for a more closed and clannish society, the sheer anxiety of living with uncertainty—are *always* ready to explode.

The standard version in which Hitler's rise—and yes, let us go back to that case and not avoid it, because it is the most acute case of a typical illness—was the result of the hyperinflation in Germany is one that everyone has heard. But the inflation was well over by the time he came to power; the anxieties might have still been there, but it wasn't the immediate or even the proximate cause. It's quite clear that there is economic anxiety in Akron, but the proximate cause of Trumpism is not economic anxiety in Akron. It's rooted in profound racial resentments and in attitudes that you can trace right back, demagogue by demagogue, to the aftermath of the Civil War.

The history of modern times is not the history of settled, complacent liberal societies occasionally subject to populist shocks caused by their own weaknesses and inconsistencies and economic crises—just the opposite. It's the history of constant agitation against the anxieties of pluralism and social change—much deeper and more pervasive than any specific economic crisis can cause—and of a drive toward a closed and settled system to control those anxieties. The authoritarian systems have different names and flavors, but they all share a profound unease with the inconsistencies and uncertainties of an open society. The liberal settlement of the 1870s was followed by those anarchist revolts against capitalist immiseration—and then even more strongly by the overwhelming force of militarized nationalism whose goal in the years leading up to 1914 was exactly to purify and regiment a liberal society that had supposedly grown too lax and decadent. (The Wilde trials were said to have shown this in England, as the Dreyfus affair had in France.) This led to the mass civilizational suicide of the Great War, which in turn was followed by the rise of left- and right-wing totalitarianisms, which dominated the life of the world for the next thirty years and were hugely popular and appealing in all Western societies, particularly to intellectuals.

Then, at the height of the Cold War, during a time of what seemed like broadly shared prosperity, the McCarthyite idea that the democratically elected government had been wholly corrupted by Communist subversion was one held by at least as many people as are true to Trumpism now. Meanwhile, the belief that racial apartheid ought to remain a permanent part of the American dispensation was held by even more. Across the ocean, Maoist ideas were wildly popular in France during its "thirty glorious years" of prosperity—even as the Chinese Communist Party starved and brutalized the Chinese. And on and on. There is no moment in that history—or at best moments no longer than a dynasty in hockey—when the settlement settled. Liberal cities and states are the tiny volcanic islands risen on a vast historical sea of tyranny.

The habits of hatred that fear creates, in Rwanda or Rouen, are *always* available to us. The plague, as Albert Camus understood, merely goes dormant for a while and then breaks out again. The question is not what ails liberalism but whatever made it whole. We have named many, if not most or all, of the causes: the confidence of educated people in their education; rising, if not generally egalitarian, prosperity; a passionate belief in pluralism; the freedom of the agora—and a few more.

History is contingent, and all we can do is struggle for sense. There lies the ultimate irony of liberalism and of liberal love stories. Liberalism is a political temperament and a credo that seeks social conciliation—one that cherishes compromise not as a reluctant last post but as a positive engine of forward movement. But the liberal is condemned and always will be to be the most embattled of all kinds.

A liberal of any complexion, my credulous kind or your more skeptical kind, Olivia, will forever be in contest with the totalitarian tendencies of the left and the authoritarian brutalities of the right. And that fight will never end. The best I can say is that you will always have allies in that struggle. You will have John Stuart Mill and Harriet Taylor, you'll have Frederick Douglass and Bayard Rustin, you'll have George Eliot and G. H. Lewes, you will have the great concert of decent humanists, from Montaigne on, stretching out behind you, assembled beside you, having fought the same kinds of fights, against much longer odds than we can now imagine, with their words and ideas and arguments and jokes and journals, as you're fighting now.

⤬

No wise liberal has ever thought that liberalism is all of wisdom. The reason liberals like laws is because they give us more time for everything in life that isn't law-like. When we aren't fighting every minute for minimal rights, or reasserting our territory, or worrying about the next clan's claims, we can look at the stars and taste new cheeses and make love, sometimes with the wrong person. The special virtue of freedom is not that it makes you richer and more powerful but that it gives you more time to understand what it means to be alive.

Liberalism isn't a political theory applied to life. It's what we know about life applied to a political theory. That good change happens step by step, stone by stone, and bird by bird, that we advance in life by invisible thoroughfares and, feeling our way along in their darkness, awaken to find ourselves changed and, sometimes, improved. That what we don't know is larger than what we do know, but that what we do know is just deep enough to trust. This working connection between the life we live and the social practice we undertake is the real hidden strength of the liberal tradition.

Liberalism is blessed and continues to produce those thousand small sanities in often invisible social adjustments and improvements, moving us bit by bit a little bit closer to a modern Arcadia. And liberalism is doomed and may be crushed at any time by its own inability to stop the stampede of unicorns that we call the utopian imagination. The work of liberalism is the work of empathy and argument, of making specific choices and particular distinctions—telling real things from imagined ones and useful ones from useless ones, rhinos from unicorns. No rule guarantees its success. It is the work of a thousand small sanities communicated to a million sometimes eager and more often reluctant minds.

If there is any comfort in its possible extinction, it's that the practice of telling false likenesses from true ones, good coin from bad—frequently in the company of people we can't stand—is fundamental to living in the real world at any moment. Empathy and argument are foundational to existence. That's why the prehistory of liberalism is mostly the history of commonplace civilization, of bazaars and agoras and trading ports—all those enforced and opportunistic acts of empathy, where you had to make bargains and share selling space and find workable commonalities with people fundamentally unlike yourself in order to live at all. That's the work of liberalism, and even if the worst happens, as it may, it is work that won't stop, can't stop, because it is also the real work of being human.

A PAGE (OR TWO) OF THANKS

Dan Gerstle, of Basic Books, approached me shortly after the 2016 election, having read my writing in *The New Yorker* on liberal people, to see if he could cajole me into a brief book about liberal ideas. This book is that book—though I'm sure he was somewhat startled, not to say shocked, by how perilously unbrief it became and how much it remained about liberals at length rather than liberalism in miniature. I thank him for the idea, for finding a title buried among many stray aphorisms, and for his beautiful care with the flow of concepts and the shape of chapters.

Henry Finder, my editor for the past twenty-five years at *The New Yorker*, oversaw and in many ways inspired my many essays on liberal thinkers and actors, which provided the seed ground—and sometimes the transplanted flowers—of so much of this book. With much in him of ironic Burkean liberalism, he gave this earnest Mill-minded liberal both inspiration and sometimes a good oppositional grinding stone to sharpen his wits against. Though I spared him having to read its many iterations, his mind and intelligence is still stowed away somewhere in this book, though probably not sufficiently. David Remnick, *The New Yorker*'s majordomo, field manager, and mentor for the past twenty years, remained unduly patient with a writer who kept telling him, loudly, that a national emergency had arrived. By making *The New Yorker* a magazine of political conscience, he has helped shape the sound of decency now for a generation.

I thank him for that, and for his friendship, now of such long date. So many others at *The New Yorker*—especially the now gaily departed and ever-missed Ann Goldstein, who superintended so many sentences—played some part over the decades in turning my jumpy thoughts into a river of words. I thank them all.

Lara Heimert and the entire team at Basic Books jumped in, and up, with what was, for me, touching and hugely supportive alacrity in making this book happen to an absurdly tight schedule. At *The New Yorker*, many diligent fact-checkers gave this book what empirical polish it has—particularly Dennis Zhou, who, in his free time, checked all that had not been checked before. I thank as well my amazing apprentice-assistant Moeko Fujji and, latterly, her successor, Zach Fine. And as ever, the evergreen Andrew Wylie, my literary agent and adviser now for thirty-five years.

Dedicating this book to my children, Luke and Olivia, may make them sound like passive recipients of this long exercise in paternal sapience, or dad-splaining. In fact, they were wholly engaged participants in it, correcting my absurdities and sharpening my vision, both politically (Olivia) and philosophically (Luke) in countless specific ways. Their imprint is all over this book, and I have never enjoyed anything more in life than narrating the proposed contents of each chapter to them over a single summer month, with coffee in our mugs and the recorder on the table between us and skeptical looks fixed on their faces. They always have had my love; now they have all my gratitude. I thank Patrick Donovan as well, one of the amazing generation of friends and readers who they have introduced me to.

Martha Parker, as she has for so long, read every page, listened to every thought, and shared completely in the construction—and cumulative exhaustions—of this book, all the while engaged in even more exhausting creations of her own. She also imagined its cover. But then she has always done all that. She has also spent a lifetime teaching me, and her world, that militant feminism and womanly love are the same things seen at different moments. It's a liberal lesson.

Two men sadly passed haunt these pages as well. André Glucksmann in Paris, whose humanity and passion always acted as a chide to my own perplexities, and Tony Judt in New York, whose acerbic clarity was always an acid to my sweeter tastes. I don't know if they ever met, or would have agreed on much—the sonorous abstractions of French humanism and the acid particularities of British empiricism are not always happy when paired—but taken together they represented the individuality and intractability that make liberal humanism human. And they both showed immense courage in the face of mortality and put their children first. I hope that neither would be too exasperated by what they read here.

A BRIEF
BIBLIOGRAPHIC NOTE

This short book is the end product of a long lifetime's reading of philosophy, history, and biography. It's also a kind of distillation and a reduction, in the cook's sense, of ideas and themes I've explored in the many, usually longish, *New Yorker* essays I have written about liberal (and antiliberal) thinkers and actors over the past twenty-plus years. These include essays on: Frederick Law Olmsted (March 31, 1997), James Boswell (November 27, 2000), Karl Popper (April 1, 2002), Voltaire (March 7, 2005), Benjamin Disraeli and William Gladstone (July 3, 2006), G. K. Chesterton (July 7, 2008), J. S. Mill (October 6, 2008), Samuel Johnson (December 8, 2008), Winston Churchill (August 30, 2010), Adam Smith (October 18, 2010), the crisis of American incarceration (January 30, 2012, and April 10, 2017), Edmund Burke (July 29, 2013), freethinkers and the theocratic imagination (February 17 and 24, 2014), Michel Houellebecq (January 26, 2015), André Glucksmann (November 11, 2015), Hitler and *Mein Kampf* (January 12, 2016), Michel de Montaigne (January 16, 2017), the morality of the American Revolution (May 15, 2017), Philip Roth on patriotism (November 13, 2017), the great crime decline (February 12 and 19, 2018), Charles de Gaulle (August 20, 2018), and Frederick Douglass (October 15, 2018). Almost all of these were, in turn, occasioned by the publication of books, often new biographies, whose virtues (and defects) are named and particularized in the essays. Almost all of these essays, along with a fuller description of the other background reading they reference and gratefully draw from, can be found in full on the *New Yorker* website (newyorker.com).

As I remark in the opening chapter, the history of liberalism has only recently been liberated from an undue midcentury narrowness. For the broader new scholarly background in thinking about liberalism and its history, I was grateful for Colin Bird's *The Myth of Liberal Individualism* (Cambridge University Press, 2007), which does much to separate Mill in particular from the myths around him, and to Anthony Appiah's *Cosmopolitanism* (W. W. Norton, 2007) and *The Ethics of Identity* (Princeton University Press, 2004) for their sections on nineteenth-century liberal nationalism particularly and for his positive take on positive liberty, or soul-making within the liberal tradition. As I was writing this book, Helena Rosenblatt's remarkable *The Lost History of Liberalism* (Yale University Press, 2018) appeared, which cheered me greatly both by its general agreement and by the many rich new instances and examples, chiefly drawn from nineteenth-century French sources, she provides in emancipating the history of liberal thought from narrow questions of rights and individualism. Emma Rothschild's *Economic Sentiments* (Harvard University Press, 2002), which I praised at length in my essay on Adam Smith, is still an eye-opener in its originality and clarity. Behind any take on liberalism and its discontents, two classic mid-twentieth century texts surely haunt the mind: Isaiah Berlin's *Four Essays on Liberty* (OUP, 1969) and Karl Popper's *The Open Society and Its Enemies* (Princeton University Press,

1971—though originally published in London in 1945). To which one should add—though I don't discuss it directly in these pages—the classic midcentury account of liberal perplexities and a much-hailed solution to many of them, John Rawls's *A Theory of Justice* (Harvard University Press, 1971).

In the opening chapter on what liberalism is and means, the material on George Eliot and G. H. Lewes draws on many sources, including, most important, Rosemary Ashton's biography of Lewes, *G. H. Lewes: A Life* (Clarendon Press, 1991), as well as his now sadly out-of-print *On Actors and the Art of Acting*, which I read (and re-read) in a Grove edition from 1962. By far the best and most recent analysis of the relationship between Eliot and Lewes can be found in Philip Davis's *The Transferred Life of George Eliot* (Oxford University Press, 2017). For Habermas's theories of social capital, the classic source is his *The Structural Transformation of the Public Sphere* (MIT Press, 1991), and for Robert Putnam on social capital, the classic source is his *Democracies in Flux: The Evolution of Social Capital in Contemporary Society* (Oxford University Press, 2004). For Bayard Rustin, the best books are John D'Emilio's biography *Lost Prophet* (University of Chicago Press, 2004) and *I Must Resist: Bayard Rustin's Life in Letters* (City Lights, 2012).

Thinking about the right-wing assault on liberalism, I drew, of course, on Berlin's *Three Critics of the Enlightenment* (Princeton University Press, 2004) and on the many writings of Charles Taylor, most particularly his *A Secular Age* (Harvard University Press, 2007). Patrick Deneen's *Why Liberalism Failed* (Yale University Press, 2017) is a most provocative recent account of the spiritual crisis perceived in the liberal dispensation. For the left-wing assault, I drew on many sources. Adam Hochschild's 1998 *King Leopold's Ghost* is the best account of the Congo genocide. Emma Goldman's wonderful memoirs, which one can now find in an (abridged) edition from Penguin Classics (2006). Also, her lover Alexander Berkman's *The ABC of Communist Anarchism*, which I read (in a library) in its original 1929 edition from Vanguard Press. Marxist and post-Marxist theory comprises too vast a list of titles to be neatly enumerated here—the significant books on culture and politics by and about the Frankfurt School alone are too enormous to list—but for contemporary theory, particularly the theory of intersectionalism, I learned most from *Critical Race Theory: The Key Writings That Formed the Movement*, edited by Kimberle Crenshaw, Neil Gotanda, Garry Peller, and Kendall Thomas (The New Press, 1995) and from Kimberle Crenshaw's many articles, now collected freshly in *On Intersectionality* (New Press, 2019), as well as from the many books of bell hooks (Gloria Jean Watkins), including her *Ain't I a Woman* (Routledge, second edition, 2014).

Finally, I'm sure that the finale of this book is illuminated by the many writings on liberalism and the pragmatist tradition by Richard Rorty, including his belatedly famous *Achieving Our Country* (Harvard University Press, 1999), and from the countless musings on the same subject—liberalism, pragmatism, and their mutual discontents—by my dear friend and *New Yorker* colleague Louis Menand.

ABOUT THE AUTHOR

Adam Gopnik is a staff writer at *The New Yorker*; he has written for the magazine since 1986. Gopnik has three National Magazine awards, for essays and for criticism, and also a George Polk Award for Magazine Reporting. In March of 2013, Gopnik was awarded the medal of Chevalier of the Order of Arts and Letters. The author of numerous bestselling books, including *Paris to the Moon*, he lives in New York City.